Hidden Treasures
in
Secret Places

Treasures are every
where —

John Hogan

Hidden Treasures in Secret Places

Velma Hagar

Disclaimer: References to Scripture are the author's paraphrase.

Editor: Jennifer Miller, www.strengthsway.com
Cover Photo: Stacey Mills
Book Design: Authorsupport.com

ISBN: 978-0-9981828-1-0

Printed in the United States of America.

Dedication

I DEDICATE NOT only this book but my exciting life's journey to my mother, Gladys Baio Hagar, and her amazing offspring, who are my siblings and have traveled this incredible life's journey with me. My sweet sister and lifetime friend, Bobbi Hagar Harrell, who has always been there for me and who has set a wonderful example as a wife and mother. She is truly my best friend in the whole world. Every girl needs a brother like Bob Hagar Jr., who has always stuck by me through thick and thin. What a guy! Last, but not least, the "Red Rocker" Sammy Hagar, our baby brother, for his generosity to the family and for adding a whole new meaning to the name Hagar.

I would also be remiss if I did not recognize and acknowledge my three wonderful, godly children:

My firstborn, my daughter and friend who has taught me as much as I have taught her and is the apple of my eye, Stacey Suzanne Mills. My oldest son, Eric Anthony Solis, who is my confidant, my mama's boy, my mentor, and my greatest admirer. My youngest son, Gregory Robert Solis, who is every mother's dream—a man of ethics, strength, and success. Thank you, sweet family.

Foreword

ONE OF MY favorite poems, "Reliance," written by
Henry Van Dyke, says,

> Not to the swift, the race:
> Not to the strong, the fight:
> Not to the righteous, perfect grace:
> Not to the wise, the light.
> But often faltering feet
> Come surest to the goal;
> And they who walk in darkness meet
> The sunrise of the soul.

I think somehow that's what Velma has been trying
to say with her devotional writings—that in each of
us lives something good enough to survive and that
we need but to believe in ourselves. Velma knows and
understands the darkness; coming from a dysfunctional
family with a violent, alcoholic father, we lived with fear.
It was our mother who first introduced to us faith that
would sustain us in the evenings when we ran, terrified
of our father, from our home to the safety of the orange
grove. She preached to us that the Lord watched over
us, and somehow we felt protected by that fact. Our
mother wasn't really brave and yet everything she did

said otherwise. She wasn't perfect and yet everything she did was. And if ever a soul walked out of darkness into the sunrise, it was our mother.

Velma came into her faith and a commitment to it as a young adult. She began going to church and reading the bible. This led her to passages and promises where she found peace, faith, and something she could believe in—a refuge, a resurrection of self. This awareness carried with it a desire to share the wonder and peace she'd learned through faith, to face life without fear and uncertainty and to forgive ourselves for the human frailties that embrace each of us.

Cloaked in faith, her experiences became a testimony to share, to offer aid to others who struggle with the daily fears and stress of living. Starting with just a little tidbit each day that renewed her own faith and encouraged her receptive readers, she has amassed page after page of useable anecdotes and phrases from the bible and her own life that encourage and inspire.

Walking from the darkness and meeting the sunrise of her soul, Velma now offers the strength of her journey— how she made it here, this day, with this faith—and shows you how you, too, can change your life to one of peace and reward and find a path of tranquility from day to day, and much will be found renewed.

In loving retrospect, sweet sister,
Bobbi Hagar Harrell

GROWING UP IN the Hagar clan, there were four of us. Oldest was sister Bobbi, second was Velma, brother Bob Junior, and myself. The pecking order one would think was pretty much in that order, but it wasn't. Velma always seemed to end up getting what she wanted first, and even when it came to the family chores she seemed to do less and get paid the same or sometimes even more.

Why, you ask? Because she was smarter than the rest of us. She was always the drama queen, saying things like, "I'm just not feeling well. Would someone please bring me a glass of water?" She slept in the longest and would complain to the rest of us for making too much noise. She pretty much ran the show. Even though Bobbi was the boss, Velma found a way to get her own way. Whether inventing her own language, which I believe we called "dog Latin," or spelling words and saying them backward faster than we could do it forward, she's always had a brilliant mind and imagination.

One of my favorite things that I still repeat today is a poem she wrote in her early teens that said absolutely nothing. Every word was a contradiction. I once took a theme she wrote in middle school and used it for a project in 7th grade and got an A on it.

Most of you would probably think I was the oddball in the family, but without a doubt it was Velma. I'm not sure what took her so long to finally write a book, but I assure you it will entertain you and have something you can use to enlighten and enrich your life. Good job, sis.

Sammy Hagar

AS I BEGAN my search for the perfect photo for the cover of my mom's book, I found myself completely captivated by the details of the cactus and their beautiful blossoms. Then it was rocks and rock formations, the skin on the back of a lizard, the sand, so much beauty we miss by skimming quickly over a landscape. It brought me back to my childhood when life was slower, and you could hear the music of God's creation all around you. We'd spend hours lying in the grass, looking at a dandelion or a ladybug or maybe watching an airplane fly high above until its smoky trail dissipated into the crystal blue sky. Then it dawned on me: this beauty was another aspect of "the secret treasures in hidden places" that Mom would talk to us about when we went on those long walks as children. The everyday beauty that God surrounds us with to remind us that He is here with us, and that we are not alone.

The beauty of His creative hand for us to return to whenever we feel sad or hopeless, alone, or maybe even depressed. It is easy to feel God's love and the essence of who He is when surrounded by His glorious creation, untouched by the hand of man. It's pure and perfect and there for the taking by all. Even in a desert, where some may only see scrub brush and desolate landscapes and feel the scorch of the sun and dry heat. Such is life when it takes us into the seasons of valleys and deserts; don't forget to look for the "secret treasures in hidden places," because it's God's hand through those trials that make us victorious travelers in this journey of life!

Stacey Mills

FIRST, MY MOM is a seeker. Even before she knew the Lord, she was on a quest to find her spiritual self. As far back as I can remember, my mom was thinking about things from a spiritual perspective. Mom was always knocking on a door in pursuit of the truth. Many a religious folk would cringe at some of the stuff our family dabbled in during those early years of Mom seeking, but she lived out Mathew 7:7: "Seek and ye shall find," and God showed himself faithful, because today my mom is a spiritual giant!

Mom believes deeply in people, especially those she loves. If you ask anybody who knows Mom, they will tell you that she is their greatest champion, because she makes everyone feel special and loved. She has an undying belief in God's plan for you and for me, especially when things seem hopeless and it gets hard to believe in yourself. Mom is there to encourage you, and her words make you believe that everything will be okay and is all according to God's plan. Anyone who knows Mom knows they can call her in a crisis and get powerful prayer and a word of encouragement. She will drop everything for a friend in need and they will do the same for her, which is why her phone rings off the hook. She has more friends that love her than anybody I know.

My mom accepts people the way they are and is always there to offer a helping hand, even to those who spitefully use her. I am not sure how she does it, but my mom has the strength and emotional integrity to forgive people even when they do not deserve it. With Mom, all it takes is a telephone call and a genuine "I am sorry," and bygones are bygones no matter how heinous the wrong. I honestly believe that this is at the epicenter of her success and a life full of blessings. I believe that God shows her favor because of the incredible grace and forgiveness that she shows people, through a heart full of compassion, love, and generosity.

Mom knows how to persevere and she never quits;

it is not only a genetic trait but a choice. My grandpa (Mom's dad) holds the record for getting knocked down more times in a professional boxing match than any man in the history of boxing. Similarly, I watched my mom get knocked down over and over again in marriage, business, and life in general; she would stay down just long enough to get in a really good cry and then she would get back up and say, "Everything is going to be okay." I watched her take one blow after another, and she never quit. Instead, she chose to persevere and fight her way to success using every trial or failure as a stepping-stone to the future.

Mom is one of the most interesting people you will ever meet. She has an amazing personality, and her enthusiasm for life is contagious. I call her a Pollyanna, because she makes looking for the positive in things a habit. She lives her life seeing the "glass half full," and if life serves her lemons, she not only makes lemonade but opens up a lemonade stand and turns it into an opportunity.

I will close by saying that my mom will never know in this life just how much she means to me. She has always been my best friend, and I adore her and think she is the bomb! I love you, momma!!!

Eric Solis

I ONCE HEARD it said that the best way to explain the theological difference between the "sovereignty of God" and "free will" is to look back at your life or look forward into your future. In other words, when you look into the future you see free will and you see the importance of the choices you make. However, when you look back, you see nothing but God's sovereignty in your life. That was certainly the case for me and my family. When I look back at our life, I see nothing but God's hand all over it.

Unfortunately, some of my earliest memories of life were not so pleasant. During the early part of my elementary school years, my parents' marriage was beginning to fall apart. Their marriage would eventually end in divorce when I was ten years old, and I felt alone and afraid. Emotionally, financially, and spiritually things were not very good at home.

Although Mom was devastated by the divorce, God gave her the strength, courage, and perseverance to fight on, and without her fight, our family would have collapsed under the pressure. She owned a small ladies shoe store in a city where the snowbirds would clear out in the summer months. I'm not sure how we survived those times, but I know that without her strong work ethic, savvy business skills, and diligence, we didn't have a chance. Watching my mom's faithfulness with that small business for so many years modeled for us how to work hard and do the best with what you have.

I was the youngest of three, with my older brother and sister in their teens. My mom was working hard and trying to recover from the divorce. I found myself alone quite a bit without much supervision. I began hanging out with older kids that frankly were not making good choices in life. To say I was a youngster at risk would be an understatement. Although I made a lot of bad decisions during that time in my life, when I reflect back to why I didn't go off the deep end, the answer is crystal clear. First, I know God had his hand in my life, and second, I never questioned how much my mom loved me, and I never wanted to disappoint her. She did an amazing job making me feel loved, and that love became the glue that sustained me during extraordinary temptations.

Although many might think that with some of the things we went through and things we lacked financially that I feel cheated or resentful, but that is not the case! As crazy as my childhood was, I feel blessed and honored to be part of God's story. It really has been an amazing journey, and I owe a big part of that journey to my mom. Today I have a beautiful wife, three precious children, and a thriving business. God has blessed me beyond measure. Make no mistake about it, there are things I learned from my mom and dad of what not to do, but there are so many things I have learned that have helped mold me into who I am today.

Although I am still a work in progress, I am very

grateful for the things I have learned from my mom when I was young and even today. The wisdom she has gathered over many years and is now sharing with everyone through this book is a testament to her love and genuine concern for others. I'm sure after reading this book, you will understand why I am so appreciative of my mom. Thanks, Mom—may God continue to give you His wisdom, and may we all continue to learn from you.

Greg Solis

Introduction

"I will give you hidden treasures, riches stored in secret places, so that you may know that I am the Lord"
(Isaiah 45:3 NIV).

HIDDEN TREASURES IN secret places—I just love it! I learned this very early in life, but it wasn't because I read it in the bible. I learned it from my little Italian mother, Gladys Baio Hagar, who brought this alive to us as we walked out in our poverty-stricken world, a world of lack and fear, fueled by a psychotic, alcoholic father. Mother insisted to my three siblings and me that not only did every single dark cloud have a silver lining but also to keep our eyes glued to the ground as we walked, because there were treasures everywhere that could easily be missed. There were treasures that others had dropped, or maybe a rock laden with gold would be found. The highlight of our week was the garbage dump where we rummaged for hours searching for usable items that were scrubbed clean, fixed, and put to use. The local potato fields often found the Hagar clan gleaning the dirt in search of the potato treasure that was left behind by the field hands. Or we were hunched over a hidden stream of water, luring the crawdads within to latch onto our makeshift fishing line consisting of string and a safety pin. These hidden treasures were often paired with our productive search in the fields alongside the Southern California highways for the tender mustard greens that were miraculously turned into a meal fit for a king. We were taught that treasures were everywhere and that God would take care of us no matter what happened. This was the belief that we all clung to. We were not allowed to be ashamed of what we had.

I remember when I was fifteen years old and we had gotten an old car. My mother was so happy and proud of it. We were driving down the street when my sister and I saw some kids from school. We ducked because we were ashamed of that old car and did not want anyone to see us in it. Mother pulled over to the side of the road and yelled out the window, "Bobbi and Velma Hagar are in this car!" She then turned to us and said, "Don't ever be ashamed of what we have, because we are so blessed to have this car." That was just one of many stories of our learning process.

I think all four of us have grown up still expecting and looking for those treasures that are scattered along the path of everyday life. Treasures often go unnoticed and unclaimed. In my mid-adult life, I began to study the bible. When I found the scripture that said, "I will give you hidden treasures in secret places," I realized that my mother did not make this up. I was thrilled and began my quest to find the hidden treasures that were throughout the Word of God. As I began to apply them to my life, I learned that I would only find them when I looked for them.

These amazing gems began to heal the scars from living in a dysfunctional home. It was a life that was filled with fear. I was afraid of everything that moved. As a young mother, I sat in the car with my three children when it rained because I had heard that the tires protected you from being struck by lightning. My neighbors were appalled. I suffered with generalized anxiety and panic attacks. I realize now that I had post traumatic stress disorder, caused by the fear instilled in me by my combative, abusive father. When I found the hidden treasure that said, "Call unto me and I will deliver you from all your fears," I did exactly that. Little by little every fear was removed. Today I am a brave, strong woman, and I thank God for this incredible transformation. My biggest fear today is not pleasing God!

Since I began to delve into the bible, I have found that there are hidden treasures in every single thing in life. There's a hidden treasure in yourself, your friends, your children, and your husband or wife. There are hidden treasures in the landscape. Some can look at the desert and see nothing but sand and tumbleweeds, but I have found many hidden treasures within the beautiful desert where I live. Be sure to watch for the hidden treasures in your life, because they are everywhere, and it is your responsibility to unearth them. My secret is this: You won't find treasures if you don't look for them, and once you find them you must appreciate them to discover more.

I wanted to share with my family and friends what I had learned about the over six thousand treasures and promises that were hidden within the pages of Scripture. So I began to send a text containing one of these pearls every morning to my children and a few close friends. From that small group, more and more friends were added to my growing list of recipients. In 2011 I began to put my blog on Facebook, and just as God promises, if you are faithful with a little, you will get a lot. My blog readers began to grow at an alarming rate. I have been asked over and over to put these little pearls of wisdom into a book. Even though I have always had a "quill behind my ear," I had never given much thought to a book.

As I entered my seventies, my audience began to grow. I told God, "If you want me to write a book, you will have to drop it in my lap." So he did! He sent one of my readers, Jennifer Miller, who is a Life and Business Coach by profession, to come all the way from Minneapolis to the desert where I live to tell me that she would help create the book by extracting the blogs from Facebook which I have been faithfully posting for over five years. She said she would edit them and put the book together for me.

It was an offer I could not refuse, and from that

Hidden Treasures in Secret Places was born. My prayer is that you will glean inspiration from the pages of this book and begin the exciting search for your own "hidden treasures in secret places." Enjoy!

January

EVERY NEW YEAR brings with it an opportunity for a brand-new, clean slate, forgetting those things that are behind and looking toward those things that are ahead. As you make your New Year's resolution, be sure to include God. Resolve to do what the Bible says and remember that all those wonderful promises only belong to you if you call him your Lord. If you haven't made that decision, the new year is a perfect time to start fresh with Jesus at the helm.

FORGETTING THOSE THINGS that are behind and looking to those things that are ahead. Think of each day as a new beginning and a clean slate. Although memories are sweet and wonderful, they are not intended to fill up our present day. Every year has its own special ambiance, and it is important that we savor the moment rather than longing for the old familiar things. Embrace each day with a new zest and reach expectantly toward the new year with new ideas and fresh resolutions.

THERE IS A passage in the Bible that talks about "hidden treasures in secret places." I just love that scripture, and I often ask God to reveal those treasures to me. Most times the treasure is right in front of us and we miss it. Sometimes we get so busy looking for the treasure that is "out there somewhere," that we miss what is right under our noses. Keep your eyes open today as you acknowledge God and ask him for "hidden treasures in secret places."

A PROMISE IS a declaration or assurance that one will do a particular thing, or that a particular thing will happen. God has given his children over 6,000 promises, but they don't just fall out of the sky. Most promises have a caveat—a condition connected to it. The condition is that we believe God's Word and obey it. We also must know what the promises are so we can look for them; they are hidden treasures throughout the Bible. "Study to make yourself approved."

DAY 3 January 3

DO YOU WANT a bigger, better, more prosperous life? Take care of and be faithful with what you already have! If you don't keep your own car clean and take good care of it, you will always drive that exact same kind of messy car, never getting anything better. And if you are slothful with your property and the property of others, God will never entrust you with very much. You will always just muddle through life with little. But "when you are faithful with a little, you will become ruler over much."

DON'T LET NEGATIVE people stop you. There are always naysayers, and they do not wish you well. They may even be family or the people you love. This does not mean they are bad people; it is just the "fallen man" syndrome. The key is to push through to your dreams anyway. Use God's Word as your guidepost toward success. He says he will show you "hidden treasures in secret places." I love that!

DAY 4 January 4

THE GIFT OF giving is not just about material stuff. We all love presents, and that is not wrong, but there's so much more to giving: the gifts of encouragement, kindness, gentleness, or understanding. Even the gift of listening to others makes them feel important. Let's remember to freely give those gifts that you cannot buy, those unique, individual gifts that only you can share with others. "He who blesses others will himself be blessed."

THINGS HAPPEN. Trust God enough to not have to know "why." Instead of asking God why, choose to trust him. Even though God is not the one who brings bad things into your life, he can and does weave it into the beautiful tapestry that makes up the whole of your life. He works everything for good for those who love him, and as you trust him, some of the worst things that have happened in your life can create the most beautiful part of your own personal life tapestry.

DAY 5   January 5

ALWAYS DO THE right thing even when it's hard. When you do what is right, it lifts and encourages you and others. Sometimes it is so tempting to tell a "little lie" or put a "small something" in your pocket or spread a "little gossip," but wrong is wrong no matter how innocent it may seem. And everything you do comes back on you. Always do the right thing!

THE WORDS *give thanks* appear many times in the Bible. When you can find things to be thankful for, God will work those bad things that happened to you into a circumstance that will work toward good for you. This does not mean that the bad things will not still be bad—they will—but it says that if we can find things to be grateful for, and give thanks, these bad things will work toward good for us. Make a life-changing decision today to be grateful, and then watch what God will do with a grateful heart. "In all things give thanks."

DAY 6   January 6

YOUR PASSION WILL lead you to your purpose. If you are really seeking God, pay attention to what you are passionate about because it is probably God urging you in a particular direction. Don't settle for a ho-hum life. Go for the things that really bless you and that you find interesting and intriguing. These are the areas where God has gifted you, and you'll always be more successful at the things that are in your sphere of interest. God's Word promises us that "he will work in us to will and to do his good pleasure."

ABILITIES ARE NOT what build your legacy; what you do with your abilities does. A legacy is built at the intersection of activity and ability. Abilities can be very mediocre but if they are used properly they can bring about an amazing legacy. Some gifted and talented individuals may end up leaving nothing behind because of their lack of activity.

DAY 7   January 7

WHEN YOU ARE afraid that things will not work out the way you hoped or imagined, just be silent. Silence is a space in which God can bring truth that will overcome assumptions. Sometimes we get so busy blabbing that we can't hear God or even other people, for that matter. I love the scripture that says, "Be still and know that I am God." This is one I personally have to work on all the time. How can you hear God when you keep talking? All you hear is yourself. Set aside a special time every day that you sit quietly and listen to God. I promise you will hear him—not with your ears but in your spirit.

WHEN YOU BEGIN your day with a quiet prayer, you will find that life will flow toward your daily goal. There will be a gentle nudging that guides you throughout the day. Make this important commitment and watch your life change. When possible, pray with a loved one. There is power in agreement!

DAY 8   January 8

YOU NEVER SO touch the ocean of God's love as when you forgive and love your enemies. It is easy to love your friends and the pretty, lovable people, but when you choose to love and forgive those who are unlovable and who have even hurt you, you touch the heart of God and bring a blessing upon yourself. God not only is love but the embodiment of forgiveness. "Those who show mercy will have mercy shown to them." I don't know about you, but I need and covet mercy!

THE BIBLE SAYS, "Do not fret—it only causes harm." And the words *fear not* are in the Bible 365 times—once for every day of the year. It seems God is pretty adamant about not fearing and fretting. When we spend our precious time fretting and fearing over things we cannot do anything about, we are actually making things worse. While it is not always easy to not worry, if we can get into the Word of God and pull out the promises that pertain to your situation and call them out to God, I promise you, peace will prevail. "Call unto God and he will deliver you from all of your fears."

THE PROMISES OF God are not self-fulfilling. A promise of God is his divine intention for your life, but unless you can believe for it yourself, you will not receive it. You will never get into the promised land God has for you until you believe you can do it. Many of God's promises go unfulfilled because of lack of faith.

WE GET A chicken by hatching the egg, not by smashing the egg to get the chicken out. "There is a time and a season for everything under the sun." And that timing belongs to God. "When you have done all you know to do, wait on the Lord." I believe that many times we either haven't done all we know to do first before we wait, or we try to rush the ripening season. There is a fine line here. Be sure you have done all you know to do before waiting, and if you think of something else to do while you're waiting, DO IT! Just keep in mind it is in God's timing, not yours.

DAY 10   January 10

GRATITUDE TO GOD should not be situational. No matter what is going on in your life, you can always be grateful because there is always something for which to give thanks. Remember during the seasons in your life that are not terrific, good times are just around the corner. Give God thanks in everything. Remember, when you praise God, heaviness and depression lighten and you feel better.

IF YOU LET your defenses down, your flesh will always choose the lower, carnal things that eventually lead you to destruction. We are living in a time when "anything goes" and can become desensitized to the raging immorality, violence, and sensationalism that we're subjected to on a daily basis. Keep your guard up to maintain the form of godliness that we are called to.

Day 11   January 11

WE OFTEN HEAR people say that all things work together for good. But it is not complete unless we add the rest of the scripture...and it says "all things work together for good to those who believe and love God and are called according to his purpose." All things DO NOT work together for good if you are not serving God and trusting in him! It does not mean that you have to be perfect, but it does mean that you must believe in and love God. This is undoubtedly one of the most valuable promises given to those that serve God.

LIFE IS NOT all about you! In fact, self-centered people are unhappy people! The more you focus on yourself and your problems, the more magnified troubles become. Try looking outside yourself and consider others more important. When you do this, you will be amazed at the joy it brings.

DAY 12   January 12

ALWAYS VALUE PEOPLE! Look them in the eye, thank them for serving you, say hello, smile, touch them in some way. Just notice them or engage them in a friendly conversation! A real blessing comes when we love the unlovely.

A CALM SPIRIT is a sign of wisdom and understanding. It is also a sign of someone who knows God is in control and that everything is going to be all right. Though there are many different kinds of characters, and some are high energy by nature, it is still possible to remain calm and confident when chaos abounds and you are heavy-laden. When you really understand and trust in God's promises, you just know that no matter what the circumstances are, you are able to cast your burdens upon God because "his yoke is easy and his burden is light." And he cares for you.

DAY 13   January 13

IT IS NOT okay to be rude or disrespectful to a parent. God's Word says that we are to honor our parents that it may go well with us. He does not make any exceptions. It does not say honor them unless they are jerks. This is not always easy. Ask God to help you honor a parent who outwardly does not seem to deserve it. He knows your struggle. Never bad-mouth your parents. In so doing, you are bad-mouthing your own bloodline. Find the good in them and focus on that.

IF YOU JUDGE others, you'd better duck, because judging is a boomerang that will come back on you like a Mack® Truck. Even if you feel qualified to judge, don't! Instead of judging, try to reconcile the areas of trouble. Leave the judging to God. Men are God's battle, not ours.

DAY 14   January 14

GOD SAYS HE will not withhold any good thing to those who walk up rightly. That is a pretty powerful promise. Sometimes it may seem that crooked, mean-spirited people are prospering while the upright are struggling, but in the end, good will always prevail in God's kingdom! Make your choice to always do what you know to be right, and then trust God to bring good things your way. "Delight yourself in the Lord and he will give you the desires of your heart."

THE ESSENCE OF sin is arrogance or a lack of humility, and without humility God's blessings do not fall on a person. Someone can be loaded with worldly goods, but without the blessing of God they are never satisfied. They will have a lifetime of lack and always be striving for more. Without God, wealth can bring many sorrows, but when God blesses, it is always enough and always fulfilling. Remember that wealth is not just material; it includes every aspect of life. "God resists the proud but gives grace to the humble."

Day 15   January 15

GOD DID NOT give us a spirit of fear but of joy and power and of a sound and well-disciplined mind. There are over 2,000 fears known to mankind, yet babies are born with only two known fears: falling and loud noises. Everything else is learned behavior. If you are experiencing fear, it is not from God. In fact, God says, "Call unto me and I will deliver you from all of your fears." When I was young, I was riddled with fears. But when I began to claim this promise, it really worked! Today I am as brave of a woman as I know. Praise God!

WHEN YOU ARE involved in a dispute with a loved one or friend, don't just sweep it under the rug. Say you are sorry and discuss your part in the problem. Sometimes it's not your fault; you might even be a victim. But if you will simply say, "For whatever part I played in our problem, I am so sorry," you will be released from the bondage that unforgiveness causes. *I am sorry* are huge words that can prevent world wars! NEVER withhold these words. They are a healing balm to every relationship.

IT'S IMPOSSIBLE TO complain and trust God at the same time. If you really are trusting God, you will have peace no matter what the circumstances look like. God does not change and is not moved by your circumstances. Complaining is a lack of faith, and without faith you cannot please God. Only believe!

YOU WILL RECOGNIZE a person of true integrity because their words and actions will always be aligned with their values. A person of integrity can be depended upon to always be fair and do what is right even when it does not benefit them. They always tell the truth, they are faithful and dependable, and they respect and honor others. In general, they are part of the solution rather than part of the problem. Ask God to instill this wonderful characteristic in you. "You have not because you ask not."

DAY 17   January 17

IT IS SO unnecessary to bad-mouth others. It seems like sometimes we think it will make us look better if we say something bad about someone else, when in fact it actually makes us look ugly. Be gentle and kind to others even if you don't like them. We don't know what they might be going through or what their journey is like. We are not called to like everyone, but we are called to love everyone. And love includes respect.

WE DON'T HAVE to feel like doing what is right; we just have to do it anyway! If we let our feelings control us we would rarely do anything that is right. Our feelings will lead us to eat the whole pie! Allowing your feelings to control your life is like the tail wagging the dog. Use your intellect and your God-given sense of right and wrong to make choices, and only allow your feelings to be involved if there is a multiple choice between several right choices that can be made. "I lay before you life and death, blessing and cursing...choose life."

Day 18 January 18

THE WORD SAYS, "In this world you will have many problems, but take heart, because I have overcome the world." There is no problem that is too big for God to handle if you can truly give it to him. When we are in the throes of a situation it can feel so hopeless, but every day brings a new beginning. Do what you can to remedy your situation and then trust that God will handle his end. "And this too shall pass."

THERE IS AN intense feeling of freedom when you accept the boundaries of your own domain. We cannot fix the world or other people. Putting our time and effort into the things that we can control frees us up to do a better job of the things that are our responsibility. Keep your own space tidy and help others when you can, but stay in your own lane.

GOD HAS SHOWN us what is good, and he requires us to show mercy, love justice, and walk humbly before him. He says that these three things are all that is required of us. Always show mercy to others or God will not show mercy to you when you need it. Love justice by always being fair and walking in integrity. The last and most important one is to recognize that God is omnipotent and we are lost without him. He made it pretty doggone simple for us. Let's just do it!

NONE OF US like to feel weak or like we are not capable to do something, but God's Word says, "In your weakness I am made strong." In most cases, if we are strong in an area we do not bother to check with God first, and the arm of the flesh can make many mistakes. Yet when we feel inadequate, we are quick to turn to God. Weakness is a good place to find yourself if you are willing to trust God. In a foxhole, there is no such thing as an atheist.

Day 20   January 20

IRRESPONSIBILITY WILL TEAR a hole in your soul! Take seriously the things that are given to you. Tend your garden well and remember that "he who tends the fig tree will eat the fruit thereof." Make a sincere commitment to yourself and God to be diligent with everything in your space.

CONFIDENCE AND NEGATIVITY are polar opposites. Negativity is a choice, and you cannot have what God has for you if you're negative. Be selective in your thoughts, and do not let negativity take you down. Surround yourself with positive people and be one of those who helps others to see the good in everything. Good is always there if you choose to see it.

DON'T BE DISCOURAGED by unanswered prayers. Many times prayers take years to be answered, and sometimes they're not answered at all. Just trust that once you have asked and you have given the situation over to God, he is working on it. Keep believing and trusting that God sees the whole picture, while we only see a tiny little speck. Those who put their trust in God will never be disappointed.

VENGEANCE AND UNFORGIVENESS of any kind will block your blessings. God's Word says, "When you stand praying, forgive, so your father in heaven will forgive you." Holding ought against anyone, no matter what they have done, blocks your own prayers. God will fight for you if you let him, but if you try to get even yourself, you will probably lose. "Vengeance is mine, says the Lord." Relax, and get out of God's way. He will see justice done.

BLESSED ARE THOSE who have never seen but still believe. A blessing falls on believers! We all need a little help believing at times, but making a decision that you will believe God's Word no matter what the circumstances may look like will cause an intense blessing to fall on you. When you have seen God's work in action, it makes believing easier, but when you choose to believe no matter what, you will never be disappointed. Choose to believe that the reason for faith is Jesus and give thanks for the blessing that he brought to the earth.

NO MATTER HOW sweet you are, it is said that there are at least ten percent of people who will not like you, and many of the people in your life will not want to help you get ahead because they are jealous and competitive and instead want you to help them get what *they* want. This is just the condition of fallen humanity. Choose to rise above this ugly condition and be one of those people who are willing to support others, and cling to the few people in your life who really want to see you succeed.

DAY 23   January 23

THERE ARE TIMES in life that the brook just dries up. This does not mean you have done something wrong; it just means that God is moving you on. If you have really done all you know to do, and things are still not working, make a slight change in your direction, or maybe even an about-face. While I do not believe in giving up on certain things, I do believe that sometimes God will make these changes in our lives. Remember, if you are truly trusting God, he will bring you to the fullness that he has for you if you are willing to let him direct your path. Let go and let God.

GOD'S REQUIREMENT FROM us is "to do what is just, to love mercy and to walk humbly before God." The simplicity of this is to always be fair and merciful to others, to always do the right thing, and to know that you are nothing without God. This is all he really requires of us. Pretty doggone easy!

Day 24   January 24

THE BEST WAY to make your dreams come true is to wake up! Daydreaming will get you nowhere. God says "he will bless the work of your hands." Sitting around waiting for God's blessings is not how it works. Acknowledge him first and then get moving! He promises to direct your steps.

NEVER GIVE UP on your dreams or on people. It is never too late for a dream to be fulfilled. Live your life to its absolute fullest right till the end, even as your body ages. Sometimes we put limits on ourselves for whatever reason, especially as we get older. The Bible says that Moses was 120 when he died, and his energy had not abated and his eyes had not grown dim. What God does for one he will do for another, so I'm going for it!

YOUR VALUE DOES not decrease based on someone's inability to see your worth. Do not allow the opinions or actions of others to make you feel inadequate. Your own opinion about yourself is very valuable for your success. God made you special, and you need to make sure that you know and appreciate who you are. Instead of comparing yourself to others, concentrate on fluffing up your own special, unique character.

ENJOY THE JOURNEY, not just the destination. Celebrate all the way to the finish line. Enjoy the process and celebrate the little successes along the way. God fills our lives with hidden treasures and sweet surprises if we don't get so busy running to our perceived place of celebration that we miss them. Relax and savor the moment even in the midst of trials. Think of everything as a new adventure. Life is really pretty sweet!

DAY 26   January 26

YOUR DECISIONS WILL make the difference between you and the one who fails and the one who succeeds. It is not your talent, nor who your parents are or where you were born or how much money you were born with; it is simply your choices. A simple "Help me, Jesus" whispered at the start of each new day can change your life!

EVERY DAY IS a new day and brings special new blessings. Be expectant as you enter into your day; don't bring your old ugly stuff from yesterday into this fresh, beautiful morning. Every day has its own issues to deal with, and God promises us that "we will have strength sufficient for the day."

IT IS NOT wrong to doubt. Life is filled with things that cause us to wonder, but it is wrong to stay in doubt and not trust God through it. Sometimes the more bizarre something seems might simply have God's fingerprint on it. God's ways are so much higher than ours, and it is difficult for us to understand them sometimes. In these moments, just trust and walk it through; it is not necessary to know all the details of the process.

GOD'S WORD SAYS, "I wish above all things that you should prosper and be in good health even as your soul does prosper." There is a difference between surviving and thriving. Just because you have escaped the real traumas of life and are just getting by does not mean you are prospering. I believe that God wants his people to thrive. As you study the Word of God and your soul begins to prosper, the rest of your life will follow. Find his promises and claim them as your own.

Day 28   January 28

BE STRONG AND courageous. Courage is not the absence of fear; rather, it is going forward in spite of fear. It is easy to take the path of least resistance and stay in a small world, never venturing out. But if you don't stick your neck out, you will never get your head above the crowd. Step out and take a chance on your dream. If you take a chance and it doesn't work, you will have increased your learning curve. Most people do not actually succeed on their first try, so if at first you don't succeed, try, try again. The second or third try is usually successful. Go for it!

LIFE IS A journey, not a destination. Don't rush through it. Take time to revel in the precious moments that can never be replaced. Each day should have a special set of memories not to be compared to anything else. Enjoy the journey!

WHEN WE HEAR God speak, it is not in an audible voice. It comes in many ways—the wind, thunder, nature, a friend, a TV or radio show, a billboard, or a movie. It can even come out of the mouths of babes. Many times it isn't even words but something we see with our eyes. I think the very best way to hear God is to read his Word. God is not restricted to the limits of this world. "Those who look for him will find him."

NEVER RISK YOUR thoughts by giving them free reign. God's Word says to "take your thoughts captive." Bring your thoughts into that which is pure and lovely. Keep direction and remember that "as a man thinks, so he is." The carnal mind will never choose the right path. Whatever you sow into your secret thought life is what you will reap. Be intentional with your thoughts.

Day 30   January 30

JUST BECAUSE WE avoid sorrow, pain, and trouble does not mean we will be happy. The testing of faith can actually create perseverance, and perseverance causes growth. The way we handle trials will bring about blessing or cursing. Don't always look for the easy way out; sometimes just facing things can bring them to their fruition.

THERE ARE SOME things in your life that are just not going to change. This is your lot in life, and the best thing you can do is embrace it and be grateful for everything, even if some of it is not what you want. There are even some prayers that will never be answered, and you may or may not ever know why. It does no good to lament over things you cannot change. Embrace your lot in life and tell God that you accept his reasons for things and make the best out of what you have.

DAY 31   January 31

GOD BESTOWS GIFTS according to the abilities of people. God is not unfair; he just knows our character. If you max out the gifts God gives you, he will give you more. If you don't use them, you lose them! And that is the difference between the rich and the poor. Use your gifts!

THE TENDENCY OF humans is to defend themselves and point fingers at others even when they are wrong. It is selfish and childish to say, "I did it because ..." or, "I did it because they did this first." Do not defend your flesh when it does something wrong. Choose to let your spirit guide you rather than letting your flesh take over. If you are willing to admit your mistakes, they will get rectified. If you defend and hang on to them, you will have to suffer the consequences. A clean slate makes for a beautiful, uncomplicated life.

February

TAKE A REALISTIC look at your life and be aware of your limitations and abilities. You won't know what your options are if you aren't realistic. Things are not likely to fall out of the sky, and you are probably not going to get a big windfall, but God will use you and your special set of abilities to fulfill your destiny. Put your efforts toward enhancing what you already have. This is where your blessing lies!

THERE IS A tidal wave of selfishness permeating our planet. We are so blessed in America, yet we have a horrible disregard for the needy. We have become more concerned about our bank accounts, which cars we drive, and how big our houses are than caring for people who are in need. Pay your blessings forward by helping someone who is less fortunate than you. "What you do unto the least of these, you do unto the Lord."

DAY 33   February 2

HOPE IS THE golden thread that should be woven into every experience of life. Without hope you cannot have faith, because faith has to have hope to latch on to. Without faith you cannot please God. Never give up hope! Hope is a choice you make. Choose to douse discouragement and ignite your hope.

DO NOT LET your flesh control your decisions; your flesh has no willpower. It will eat the whole pie if you let it reign. Carnal thinking is simply being overconfident and making personal choices and decisions without including God. Our sufficiency should be in God rather than in ourselves. Keep balance in your life by running everything by Him first. "God loves a just and balanced weight."

DAY 34   February 3

THE CONDITION OF your heart is determined by your mouth! And not only does it expose your heart, it also brings blessing or cursing. The tongue is a little member, but it has the ability to set your life on a course of destruction! "Be careful little mouth what you say."

WE ARE NOT held responsible for subconscious thoughts, but just because a thought has not surfaced does not mean it doesn't have power to create havoc in your life. Usually subconscious thoughts will surface in small, seemingly insignificant ways. Ask God to show you any of these secret enemies that are lurking in your subconscious and then cast them out, because once you are aware of something, you are held responsible for the thought itself.

DAY 35   February 4

FAITH IS TRUSTING and believing God even when we don't know what is going to happen. It is believing for the things hoped for even when they seem farfetched. Without faith there is no hope, and without hope life becomes overwhelming. We are all given the same measure of faith at birth, and just like a muscle, if you use it, it will become buff, while a lack of use will cause it to become limp and useless. Use it or lose it!

GOD'S WORD SAYS, "If a man is skilled in his work he will stand before kings." It doesn't matter what your work is, it only matters how well you do it. If you always do your best and maintain a good work ethic all your life, in the end you will be able to count yourself successful. Remember, you shoot yourself in the foot every time you complain about your job or your boss. Work hard and be grateful.

DAY 36   February 5

LIFE CAN CHANGE in a moment's time; you can be carefree one moment, and the next moment dealing with intense stress. This is life! But if you can train yourself to keep your eyes on God and not be so particular about keeping everything in order, he promises to walk through everything with you and work it all toward good.

IN ORDER TO be really happy, you must be grateful. When you choose to see the good in everything and learn to thank God even for the trials that cause you to grow, life will be a delight. Remember, you will always find what you are looking for. "In the mud and scum of things, there always, always something sings!"

THE WORLD'S WAY of pursuing riches is grasping and hoarding, while God's way is letting go and giving. As long as you hoard and grasp, you will never have enough. Let God's natural ebb and flow operate in your life and you will always have plenty. The TV portrayal of the hoarder's surroundings is exactly what happens when we do not release things—whether it be emotions, anger, stuff, or anything in life. Be a giver!

ENCOURAGEMENT IS OXYGEN for the soul. When a person is discouraged they will not perform well, and they cannot function properly. Encourage one another and build each other up. It is not natural to be an encourager; you have to work at it. A real encourager will maximize a person's strengths and minimize their weaknesses. The biggest encouragement you can give someone is to pray for them in their hearing. Encouragement is one of the most powerful things we can do for each other.

DAY 38   February 7

FOCUS ON THE positive things in life. Do not allow yourself to sit spellbound in front of the television, listening to negative reports. For some reason sensational negativity seems to be the draw these days. Seek out and connect with the good things that are happening all around us. Don't allow yourself to get caught up in the tragedies of life. "This is the day that the Lord has made; I will rejoice and be glad in it."

"GIVE THANKS WITH a grateful heart." A grateful heart is the biggest blessing of all. You can have all the money and all the stuff in the world, but if you are not grateful, you are the poorest of the poor. And the beautiful part of this is that being grateful is a choice! There's always something to be grateful for. Stop and count your blessings, and remember to give thanks for them.

Day 39   February 8

"PERFECT LOVE CASTS out all fear." The opposite of love is not hate but fear. When we trust, we are not afraid. The more we love, and are loved, the less fear can operate in our lives. People can and will let you down, but when you allow God to be the source of your trust, he will never let you down. And I promise that if you "call unto him he will deliver you from all your fears." It may not happen overnight, but it will happen. I know because I did this! In my youth, I was riddled with fear, but today I am practically fear free! Thank you, Lord!

DON'T CHOOSE TO do life alone. There will always be traitors in your life and people who will hurt you, and sometimes it will even be family or loved ones, but do not let that sour you toward others. There are those who will support you, those who will laugh with you and cry with you and stand with you in dire times of need, those who will "stick closer than a brother." Choose to be that kind of valued friend to others, and remember that "he who has friends must show himself friendly."

COMMIT TO STAND firm against all forms of cynicism. The world is full of cynics who love to nitpick and find fault with everything. They never see anything good in anything because, frankly, they walk in complete fear. They will never encourage you because they honestly believe that you cannot achieve your dreams. If you choose to listen to these naysayers, you will never go anywhere or attempt anything. Commit to block your ears from these negative people. Remember that "God directs the steps of the righteous," and when God guides, God provides. Go for it!

GOD'S WORD SAYS, "Words aptly spoken are like apples of gold in settings of silver." Don't you just love that! Apples of gold in settings of silver. Wow! Words can have that kind of effect. And we all have the ability to do this for ourselves and for each other. Speaking words that are sweet, encouraging, positive, and uplifting can actually change a life! This is not a gift that some have and some don't; this is a gift that every one of us can and should be operating in daily. Let's do it!

DAY 41 February 10

THE HAPPIER YOU make other people, the happier you will be! Choose to consider others more important than yourself; it is one of the secrets of true happiness. Self-centered people are always miserable. If you don't like the way other people are treating you, check yourself. Your treatment of others is a boomerang that will come back on you like a Mack® Truck! Life is filled with joy when your goal is to make others feel good.

WE ARE ALL called to serve God in one way or another, and it isn't always through a church building. We can serve God from every walk of life, whether you are a pastor, financial planner, bus driver, merchant, waitress, carpenter, housewife, gardener, or whatever you do, there is a calling from right where you are. The part you are given is equal to all others. Run your race from the lane you are given and do not try to crowd others out or compete for their space. No one else can run your race for you. "Run as if to win."

DAY 42   February 11

IF WE ARE not careful, regret can turn into resentment very easily. And while it is important to recognize wrongdoings, there is no value in stewing over past mistakes. Once you have asked for forgiveness and made restitution where you can, move on—"forgetting those things that are behind and pressing on to those things that are ahead." We all make mistakes, and God is so gracious to forgive us when we ask.

THE WORLD IS full of mean-spirited people, and we are called to pray for them. It is not always easy to pray for someone that you would like to have lightning come down on and strike. But always remember that God loves everybody. He knows their hearts and the pain they are feeling. Our job is simply to pray for them. It is God's battle, not ours.

DAY 43   February 12

NEGATIVE THOUGHTS AND remarks are part of life, but never let the last thought or word be negative. Whenever these negative thoughts come, always put a positive note on it. Everything has an upside and a downside—choose to always see the upside. It is good to be realistic and know the downside, but always polish it off with an upbeat, positive note. "If there be anything of value or noteworthy, think on these things."

IF YOU ARE holding anything against someone, and you are praying and believing for something, don't expect God to bless you. If you do not forgive others, you are cursing yourself. It does not matter what they have done to you. You have to forgive them! Our perfect example is Jesus hanging on the cross and saying, "Forgive them, Lord, they know not what they do." Getting hold of this is paramount to the success of your life. Forgive!

WHEN YOU PUT perfume on others, you will always get some on yourself. Never withhold from others, because as you give to them, you are actually getting something for yourself. Giving opens the windows of heaven, whether it be money, gifts, time, or encouragement—they all bring blessings back into your life. Always choose to be an encourager. It is truly more blessed to give than to receive, and remember that whatever you do for others, God will also do for you.

OUR IMPERFECTIONS HAVE nothing to do with God's ability or willingness to hear our prayers. Those who stay close to God and communicate with him daily will be stable in all their ways and nothing will shake them. We all have something in our lives that we would like rid of, but this does not change God's love for us or his desire to bless us. Whether you are being humbled or elevated, keep looking to God and never give up! "In due season you shall have your reward."

DAY 45   February 14

GOD'S WORD SAYS, "In the mouth of two or three witnesses a truth is established." If you are seeking the will of God and you're looking for confirmation, listen for your answer to come through the mouths of others. Many times this is the way God confirms something he is trying to tell you. If you hear something twice within a short period of time, it's usually God speaking to you. If you hear it three times, listen up!

WHEN YOU FEEL like you have nothing left to give, this is when true sacrificial giving can begin. And sacrificial giving is where the big blessings lie. When we give out of our abundance, it does not have near the value that giving out of our need produces. It is truly more blessed to give than to receive. No matter where you find yourself, try giving something that someone needs, even if it is at your own expense. It enhances your life every single time!

WHEN WE LOSE something in our life, God will always replace it with something else. The problem is, most of the time we fail to notice the replacement; instead, we lament over what we lost. Be intentional in recognizing the new things that God has put in your life and focus on them, because that is where your blessings lie! "A grateful heart always has enough."

ENCOURAGEMENT IS ONE of the sweetest gifts you can operate in, and every one of us has that gift. Encouragement actually means to put courage into someone. Imagine how powerful your words can be to someone. Never withhold encouragement. When you see something nice, always say it; don't just think it. Everyone needs encouragement. Purpose in your heart today that this will be your new modus operandi!

SHEEP RESPOND TO their shepherd's voice. They will not respond to the call of strangers, but when their shepherd calls, they go toward his voice. It is much the same with God and his children. We can hear our Shepherd. It is that "still, quiet" voice that says, Stop, go this way. It is that gentle urging to do what is right. It is that calm assurance that all is well with your soul. Listen for the Good Shepherd's voice and choose to follow it all the days of your life.

IF YOU'RE TRYING to impress everyone, you will always be miserable. Give everything your best shot and believe it's good enough. There are always people that you cannot please no matter how hard you try, and we are never really free until we don't have a need to impress others. Instead, strive to please God, because when you please him, you will have favor with both God and man.

"DISHONEST SCALES ARE an abomination to the Lord, but a just weight is his delight." Cheating, lying, and unfairness of any kind is an abomination to God. He will always be on the side of truth, fairness, and justice. Those who operate any other way are bringing judgment down on themselves. Walk your life out choosing to be fair, considerate, and kind, causing blessings from God to abound in your life as you delight yourself in him.

THERE ARE TWO distinct sides to pride: one side is considering yourself more important than you should; the other side doesn't accept the beautiful person that God created. Both sides are very self-serving. Pride is pride, no matter which side you operate in, and is one of the seven things God hates most!

DAY 49   February 18

GRACIOUS WORDS ARE like a honeycomb—sweet to the soul and healing to the bones. They are actually healing to both the soul and the body. Words have such an impact on our lives and in the lives of those around us, and yet we fling words around recklessly like they mean nothing. Use your mouth to comfort, compliment, console, and encourage, and keep in mind that as you speak these sweet words, you are also receiving the benefit.

STRIVING, BACKBITING PEOPLE bring a curse on themselves and on you if you allow them to remain in your sphere of influence. Many times they are passive-aggressive. They appear to be beaten down and insecure, when in truth they have major control and greed issues. They are usually powered by envy and jealousy, and God says where these operate there is also every other evil working. Steer clear!

DAY 50   February 19

REPLACE BAD WITH good. Just as you can't put a piece of furniture in a space that already holds a piece of furniture, the same holds true in the spiritual realm. Discard the old, ugly, bad, outdated things in your life to make room for the new, beautiful, updated good things that God wants to give you. Don't clutter your life by trying to bring the new things in with the old still there. Clutter is likened to an unattended garden overgrown with thistles and weeds—ugly, unproductive and unhealthy.

NURTURE YOUR SENSE of thanksgiving. Deliberately develop a grateful heart because in so doing you will open doors for God to bring greater blessings. If you are not grateful for what you have— you don't take care of it—you will never get anything better. Grumbling and complaining is not only nonproductive, it will also stifle your blessings. "Give thanks with a grateful heart."

HAVOC AND CHAOS are a very real part of life. Choose to have compassion on the havoc in the lives of others. Life is full of potholes and choices, and many times we fall victim to the choices of others who are close to us. The main thing to keep in mind is that this too shall pass. Nothing is permanent, and if you keep going forward and trusting God, one day the wall will come down.

FORGIVENESS IS GIVEN in an instant, while trust has to be built. We are told that we must forgive, but it doesn't say anywhere that we have to trust right away or at all. When someone has deeply hurt us, it will take more than just an apology to learn to trust them again. We must accept their apology, but it is actually foolish to trust them again too quickly. Trust must be gained over a period of time to be absolute. "Be wise as a serpent but gentle as a dove."

GOD'S WORD SAYS, "Pray for one another, that you may be healed." When we pray for others, that prayer is coming right back on us and our needs will also be met. It is especially good to find someone who has your same need and pray for them. God's word is true. If he says it, that's the way it is! Pray for others that you might be healed.

CAST DOWN WILD imaginings. You cannot help it if a bad thought comes into your mind, but you can help whether you choose to entertain that thought. People who are erratic and unbalanced have usually entertained a thought that came into their head that was not good. We tend to blame our deficits on our DNA, our upbringing, or even our culture, when in fact it is nothing more than our choices. We were not born that way. Somewhere along the line we made a choice to entertain something that came into our head.

DAY 53   February 22

IN A DEFAULT mode, we tend to give the kind of love language that we need instead of learning what pleases another person. The five love languages are acts of service, quality time, physical touch, words of affirmation, and gifts.[1] While all of these can be important to every person, there is usually one that will stand out. If you take note of and operate in this special love language, you will form deeper, more loving relationships as you "consider the other more important than yourself."

NEVER TAKE THINGS for granted. If you have been blessed with the good things in life, give God thanks daily and remember that "to them that much is given, much is expected." Fame, fortune, friends, and even good looks are all fleeting and can be gone in the blink of an eye. To strive after earthly treasures is nothing more than chasing the wind. Everything under the sun is temporal, and only the things that are done for God will stick. Seek after heavenly treasures that do not fade and rust but last for an eternity.

---

1 Gary Chapman, The Five Love Languages (Chicago, IL: Northfield Publishing, 1995).

STUDIES SHOW THAT forty million people in America suffer with anxiety. Anxiety is not a sin and it is nothing to be ashamed of. Do not allow others to put their legalistic idea in your head that it is caused by lack of faith. It is not! Anxiety is a natural response when we feel threatened or overwhelmed in life. Shame and isolation will only make it worse. Short-circuit anxiety with prayer and affirmations and take a break from the big things in life. Strengthen yourself by just doing basic things, and don't lose heart. Look to God. "He gives strength to those who are weary and he gives renewed energy to the weak."

THE WORLD IS full of offenses, and if you choose to receive offenses it will stunt your growth. There is absolutely nothing beneficial in taking offense to what others have said that may or may not have been meant to insult you. If a word comes out against you that isn't true, God's Word says it will go back on the one who sent it. Be willing to give others the benefit of the doubt. It's God's battle, not yours.

Day 55   February 24

JUSTIFIABLE RESENTMENT IS still resentment. Many times we have good reasons to hold aught against someone, but we still need to forgive. Anger will rob your joy and peace and will keep you bound to whom you resent. Sometimes forgiveness is a process. Ask God for help, and "walk it out."

YOU WILL NEVER be successful unless you learn to balance work with play. If you are all work and no play, you will become grumpy and weary. If you are all play and no work, you will become hungry! God loves a "just and balanced weight," and this includes all aspects of life. Work hard and then take time to enjoy the fruit of your labor. Life is a gift. Sop up your days, leaving no regrets.

GOD KNOWS EVERYTHING about us and still loves us. We can hide things from others, and we can even hide things from ourselves, but God sees our heart and knows our thoughts, and still loves us unconditionally. Men put conditions on love, but God loves his children much like a parent loves their child, only much more magnanimously. His love has no conditions and his love is pure, noble, and forgiving. Talk with God and be honest with him; share your deepest hurts and thoughts. "Give your burdens to him and he will care for you and will not let you slip."

FEAR WILL ERODE your zeal for life and can actually paralyze you and take you hostage, to the point that you miss all sorts of opportunities and never find your way in life. Everyone has experienced or is experiencing some sort of fear, and those fears will tell you where you do not trust God. If you can redirect your focus from your fears to God, and you will call out to him, he promises to deliver you from ALL your fears. The Bible is the most powerful tool to fight fear.

DAY 57   February 26

THERE ARE ALL kinds of thievery in life. Sometimes thievery happens because of our own choices, the choices of others close to us, and sometimes we just fall victim to the myriad of crooks that live in this fallen world. But the good news is that "if a thief be found out he must repay seven times over." Remember that we are told to bring "God in remembrance of his word," so when you fall victim to an undeserved rip-off of any kind, remind God of this awesome promise and expect restitution multiplied by seven! This includes every kind of rip-off—emotional, financial, relational, physical, everything that God has given you.

BITTERNESS IS DEADLY and it will eventually defile the whole body. It is also very contagious and will affect everyone near you. A root of bitterness is like a cancer in your body that will grow and metastasize if you do not take hold of it. Never, never, never hold on to anger or unforgiveness. The only antidote for the poison that bitterness releases in your body is to give it to God. There are some issues that we really cannot do ourselves, but God can handle it. "His yoke is easy and his burden is light."

"**PLEASANT WORDS ARE** like a honeycomb, sweet to the taste and healing to the bones." Just imagine. Kind words can actually bring about healing to the bones. We need to take that scripture literally and use kind words on others. This is such a simple solution, it almost seems ridiculous that we do not take his promises to heart. Instead, we bumble through life and take all of our cares to the doctor and get a pill. God gave us an antidote in the Bible for everything, and the only reason they don't work is because we don't use them.

EACH OF US has flaws in our character, but do not accept these flaws as just being who you are. Recognize and manage your character flaws. To deny them and defend them not only allows them to operate at peak capacity, but is downright stupid and can destroy relationships. Never defend your flesh when it is out of order. Take charge of your personality and ask God to help you. Remember, "God is faithful to finish the work that he has started in you," but you have to do your part to help.

Day 59   February 28

"WHEN YOU STAND praying, forgive, so that your prayers will not be hindered." You can be sweet, you can do everything right, you can attend church every week, but if you do not forgive others, I believe this is one of the main reasons why prayers are not answered. We think we have forgiven someone because we stay away from them or don't talk about them, but we are holding unforgiveness in our heart, and God looks at the heart. Ask God to show you where any unforgiveness may be hiding, and then do what you can to make peace with that person. Ask God to help you forgive—he knows your hurt. Many times it is only God that can help you forgive and forget.

IF YOU WANT extravagant blessings, you have to be an extravagant giver. Remember that your blessings are measured by the same measure you use with others. Whether it be your time, talent, or treasure, give it generously and watch God open the windows of heaven and pour out more blessings than you can hold. Try it; it works!

March

ENCOURAGEMENT IS A powerful gift that every single one of God's children should be operating in. And when you receive a word of encouragement, rather than just saying thank you, stop and let it wash over you. Grab hold of it as if it were something tangible. Our flesh tends to go toward things it hears, especially if we stop and absorb it. Do not take words of encouragement lightly, and do not give words of encouragement sparingly. Be quick to encourage others.

DON'T MISS YOUR moment! Be alert to the opportunities that come your way. Many times something will come our way and slip by because we were too busy "chasing a lark," or watching the horizon for a fantasy. Don't miss the treasures that are right at your feet.

TREAT OTHERS THE way you want them to treat you! A nasty attitude will bite you in the butt. And don't put your expectations on others. Everyone is unique, and we all have issues that can be aggravating. Be kind and remember that "those who have friends must show themselves friendly."

IF WE NEVER take a risk we will miss out on some of our biggest blessings. It is so easy to cling to the old familiar rock. But the truth is that there are usually one of two reasons we cling to the rock, and they are both rooted in sin. Usually it is stubbornness or fear that prevents us from doing new things. Stubbornness is one of the ugliest character traits, and God actually compares it to witchcraft. We are told many times in the Bible to "fear not." So let go of the rock and try something new.

STUDIES SHOW THAT we tend to think of ourselves based on what the most important person in our life thinks of us. This can be such a troublesome situation because the favor of men cannot be trusted; it is fickle, competitive, and many times unfair. This is where the love of God can change the character of an individual. When you know how much God loves you and you are committed to pleasing him rather than man, you will find that you think you are pretty doggone special. Open your heart to the love of God—no one on earth will ever love you like God does.

IF YOU DO not accept God, you judge yourself. God responds to our trust and respect for him. God loves everyone equally, even the ignorant, but it is how we view God that makes the difference. We bless or curse ourselves by our own perception of God. God is real and he is omnipotent. Try giving him the respect due him and watch your life change.

Day 63   March 4

QUALITY TIME SPENT with your loved ones is a much-needed expression of love. Quality is not the same as quantity. Just because you are physically present with someone is not the same as quality time. Sincere, interactive communication as well as fun and laughter can be a wonderful antidote to stress and problems. If two people set their caps to "consider the other more important than themselves," life with each other will be off the charts!

GOD IS IN control, and everything plays out according to his ultimate plan. When we grasp the significance of the sovereignty of God, our cares are lessened, our hearts are calmed, our spirits are lifted, and our days are brighter. To say that God is sovereign is to declare that he is the Almighty. No one can defeat his plans, prevent his purpose, or resist his will. Relax, the battle is his, not yours!

GOD TELLS US to "be strong and courageous." This implies that we are not born with those qualities. We are all born crying little babies. Strength is a commitment we make to our own character, and while it is not always easy to do, we are called as Christians to be strong and courageous in every situation. Courage is a learned behavior.

THINK YOURSELF HAPPY and think yourself successful; everything that happens in your life begins with a new thought. "Cast down all wild imaginings" and only allow in those thoughts that are edifying and encouraging. You can actually think yourself happy! Do not allow yourself to be anything else. If it is yours, choose to love it. Whining and complaining about what you have will never bring success. Those who are content with what they have, and take care of it, will always get more.

Day 65   March 6

WHEN WE REJOICE in the prosperity of others, we give contentment to ourselves. It is the nature of the "fallen man" to compete with others and resent them when they prosper. Do not allow yourself to stoop to this carnal behavior. Instead, rejoice with them, and a wonderful sense of well-being will always follow.

THE CONDITION OF man is to see what he wants to see. But the wise man keeps his mind open and tries to see not only truth but also takes into consideration the opinions of others. Although it is not necessary to believe like someone else believes, it is both wise and courteous to consider other opinions. Sometimes you will find that something you never even thought about is actually possible, and even right. A closed mind becomes stagnant and unteachable. "Humble yourself and God will exalt you."

DAY 66   March 7

BE IN THE elite group of people who continue to grow and learn every single day. Be one who is always open to a new, better way of doing things, who continues to study to make themselves approved. Know-it-alls are a turnoff and imprison themselves in a small box of their own understanding. While it is good to stand strong on your convictions, be ready and even expectant to expand and grow no matter how old you get. If you don't bend, you will break!

IT IS IMMATURE and naive to think that we can "fix" people. While we can definitely bring added pleasure to others, it is never our responsibility to make them happy. True happiness lies in realizing that God is the source of joy. When others try to manipulate you into believing that you are the reason they are happy or unhappy, you are falling into a trap that will suck you dry. You will spend your days trying to do something that only God can do.

WE NEVER KNOW how strong we really are until we do not have any other choice. God's Word says, "He will give us strength sufficient for the day." The hardest evils of all to endure are the ones that never arrive. Fretting over what might happen is a total waste of your precious time. Enjoy the moment.

DISCOURAGEMENT WILL SHAKE your faith, and without faith it is impossible to please God. Discouragers will always abound, and if you choose to listen to them, you will never get ahead. They only look at the negative side of things and see all the things that could go wrong. Never make your choices in life based on fear, especially the fear someone else has stirred in your head. If you have a vision, let God choose for you by trusting him. "Those who put their trust in God will never be disappointed."

DAY 68 March 9

INFIDELITY HAS RUN rampant where morals have declined, and television makes it seem like it's just part of life. But God's Word says that a married man who has affairs is "like an ox being led to the slaughter" and that "he will be reduced to a loaf of bread." God's Word is true, and if you call yourself a Christian, these are grievous words.

MOST PEOPLE ARE victims because of their own choices. While it is easy to blame parents or others for our misgivings, it is usually nothing more than the choices that we make throughout our life that make or break our success. The wise man learns from and takes responsibility from past mistakes. The fool blames others and has to have a rod taken to his back!

Day 69   March 10

FEAR OF DYING is very common, even among believers. Death is a cumbersome, mysterious transition that everyone has to face, but we really have nothing to fear when we know where we are going. So relax and enjoy your chosen days, because "a man of God, in the will of God, is immortal until his work on earth is done." Run your race as if to win, savoring the journey along the way!

A SATISFYING LIFE will always come when we do things God's way. We should never just settle for the satisfactory life that comes with power, drugs, recognition, or fame. It will never be enough when we are feeding into the appetite of life. Without God's true blessing we will never feel like we have enough. God promises us a "long, satisfied life." Your choice: satisfactory or satisfied.

GOD ALWAYS SEES the heart of man and we are judged accordingly. You are not getting by with anything, even if you are acting sweet. Thoughts don't have as much power until you act on them, but once they enter your heart they will inevitably manifest, because "out of the abundance of the heart, the mouth speaks," and "from the heart comes the issues of life." Check your heart often for its motives, because therein lies the key to a blessed life.

GOD SAYS THAT "in our weakness he is made strong." Sometimes when we think we are at the end of our rope and everything looks hopeless, this is actually our strongest position, because God says that when we've done all we know to do, he will come in and do the rest. Our part is to "stand and believe." There are times in life that we have done all we can do and there is nothing left but to wait on God. "Be still and know that I am God."

DAY 71   March 12

WHEN PEOPLE BEGIN to sink in their bad choices they usually turn to prayer, but when God doesn't answer right away they get mad at him. God will always hear your prayer, but if you jump off a building and pray on the way down for God to help you, you are still going to hit the bottom. However, God's mercy will always be there when you seek him, and he can take your mistakes and the problems they have created and make something good out of them. No matter what you have done, God will surprise you with another chance if you ask.

NOT ALL YOUR questions will be answered. Life and all of its workings are a mystery, because God's ways are higher than our ways. We tend to look at things from our own puny, self-centered perspective, but things are not all about us. The whole universe is working majestically together to bring about the plans of God. Things are unfolding just as they should. Do what you know to do, trust God, and don't fret. God has a handle on it!

Day 72   March 13

THE MOST RADICAL treatment for the fear of man is the fear of God. God says that there is nothing for us to fear as long as we do what is right. "If God be for us, who can be against us?" Man's inhumanity to man has run rampant on the earth since the beginning of time, but if you do what is right and honor God, he will always fight for you and he will always see justice done. Don't just look at your current circumstances; sometimes things take years to be balanced out, but they always are in the end. Be at peace.

GOD'S WORD SAYS to "pray for those that spitefully use you." There are times that people do things to us that enrage us, but the correct response is to pray for them! There are no ifs, ands, or buts about this. If you want to get God's true blessings in life, you have to do it the way God says to do it, even if you don't understand it or it is hard to do. Always do what God says and everything else will be added unto you!

THERE IS NO denying that some people just seem to be more blessed than others. I don't claim to know the reason for that, but I do know this: God's Word is true, and he says, "I will bless those who have a heart to bless others." There are over 6,000 promises in the Bible and most of them have a caveat attached to them. God incorporates our choices into the perfection of his will. Choose to do your part to bring about God's promises in your life. Start by blessing others!

THERE ARE CERTAIN roles in life that are above your abilities. This does not mean you are inferior; it means you were uniquely created with a special set of abilities. You will know your niche because it will come easy to you, and you will do it well. Choose to run in the lane that has been designated for your life's journey. "Run your race as if to win" and be satisfied with your gifts as you strive for excellence.

PATIENT, CONSIDERATE LOVE does not come natural to man. We have to work at it. Love is a beautiful thing that can be easily destroyed by unchecked words, or even body language or facial expressions. Respect and love walk hand in hand; disrespect of all sorts can weaken a beautiful love. Make a conscious effort to always treat your loved ones with respect, and remember that even jests can be destructive if they come from a place of disrespect. "Do unto others as you would have them do unto you."

A SUDDENLY DOES not happen all at once. There is usually a lengthy process involved before a suddenly happens. Sometimes it appears that things happen in an instant, and occasionally they do, but for the most part it takes years for a suddenly to manifest. Wait and trust that throughout your life there will be many sweet surprises as you are diligent with your part in the process.

Day 75   March 16

IF YOU DON'T stop to refuel, you will burn out. It is very serious and can create all sorts of physical and emotional disorders. Discover your way to refuel. First, set aside time for prayer and to read God's Word, go shopping, enjoy a movie, have coffee with a friend or a weekend of respite away from everything. These are all good ways to refuel. Balance in everything is part of God's plan for us. "God loves a just and balanced weight," and this does not include racing through life until you burn out.

BE CAREFUL NOT to hurt people; the pain you cause can chisel away at their heart until there is no love left. Words are one of the biggest causes of pain. We have the power of life and death in our words. Train yourself to say kind things, or just shut up. Sometimes, silence is truly golden.

DAY 76   March 17

WE INTERPRET WHAT we see by what we believe. "Eyes are the window to the soul." The way you see life is directly attached to your belief system and your heart. You will see beauty and good in things when you have chosen to fill your mind with the beauty of life. If all you ever look at is disgusting, filthy, cruel, ugly things, this is how you will view the world. "Your eye is a lamp that provides light for your whole body."

"DRAW CLOSE TO God and he will draw close to you." Just because you do not "feel" God does not mean he is not there. When you choose him, he will choose you and there is no sweeter life than serving God. You do not have to earn your way; just choose him and he does the rest.

DAY 77   March 18

IT IS SAID that ten minutes of unbridled temper can waste enough strength to do a half day of wholesome work. And the poison it puts into your system cannot be healed by any antibiotic. Anger causes all sorts of maladies in your body. Refuse to let yourself go to that place of anger and ask God to help you mellow out.

PEOPLE ARE ACTUALLY stress inducers, and if you are always trying to impress or please people, you will find your stress level to be very high. Attempting to please people all the time will also cause you to compromise your core values if others think differently from you. This is especially true when you make people BIG in your life; the bigger they get in your mind, the smaller you will make God. Choose to please God rather than man and in so doing you will find that you actually have "favor with man" and a whole lot less stress.

DAY 78   March 19

GOD SAYS, "WITH whatever is in you, be at peace with all men." We all have a couple of core buttons that will set us off when pushed, and when you know what those buttons are with your loved ones, it is hitting below the belt to use them. Consider others more important than yourself and always play nice.

PASSION ALWAYS DEMANDS expression. A successful, happy person works toward using his passion to earn a living. Always be diligent to honor God as you seek to express your passion and remember that God instilled this desire in you and gave you the talent to fulfill your destiny for his glory.

WHEN REFLECTING BACK on your life, rejoice in your victories instead of lamenting over your failures. Your mistakes have helped to shape your character, and your ability to overcome has developed strength. Encourage yourself by remembering your own victories. Life is an outrageous journey filled with tons of beautiful, wonderful, exciting moments, while interspersed with many trials. When confronted with trials, walk them out and comfort yourself with hope for tomorrow, because "this too shall pass."

ALWAYS MAKE THE choice to do what is right. If you do the right thing even when things are wrong, in the end everything will turn out right. It is so easy to rationalize and defend our self-serving, self-protective choices, but I believe we were all created with an innate knowledge of right and wrong, and when we choose "right," we are choosing God. And when we "choose God and his righteousness, all other things will be added to us."

DAY 80   March 21

IF WE KNOW something is wrong and we choose to do it anyway, we are judged more harshly by God, much like a two-year-old who does something that a ten-year-old would never get away with. However, when we break spiritual laws, there will always be consequences to pay. If you run a red light, there is a high likelihood of getting hit by another car. God's laws are for our own protection.

GOD DOES NOT judge us by what we do; God judges us by why we do it. Our motive is extremely important. Even if we do something good, but our motive is out of line, God's blessing is not there. Do not do good works just to be well thought of by others. Always check your motive, because many times we even fool ourselves. However, we do not fool God, and he is the only one we really need to impress. As long as we have a need to impress others, we are never truly free.

DAY 81   March 22

KIND PEOPLE LIVE longer and stay healthier. It actually impacts your health. Kindness is love in action. Saying you love someone and not treating them right is totally out of whack. Husbands and wives, if you want a happy marriage, treat each other kindly. Don't be rude to one another. You are affecting each other's health. "Do onto others as you would have them do unto you."

BOASTING AND BRAGGING is not only unattractive, it is dangerous and ungodly. Bragging and boasting can actually cause a reversal in what we brag about. "Be careful when you think you stand lest you fall." Bragging is insinuating that you think you stand in a better position than other people, and this can cause you to fall so easily. Be grateful for what you have, but stay humble about your blessings and let God exalt you.

Day 82   March 23

THE BOOK OF James says that a "prayer prayed by someone who is living right with God is something powerful to be reckoned with." We take prayers so lightly. I think when we get to heaven we are going to be amazed at the power left unused. If you have a need in your life, seek out someone who is living right with God and ask them to get in agreement with you in prayer. "The effectual fervent prayer of a righteous man avails much."

PRAISE AND WORSHIP is not only singing; it can be as simple as saying thank you to God. Don't allow yourself to get so busy with focusing on the things that are wrong in your life that you neglect to say thank you for the things that are right. Stop and notice even small successes and forward movements. Gratefulness will always precede blessings. "Give thanks in all things."

DAY 83   March 24

KEEP A VISUAL reminder of your dreams before your eyes to keep your hopes and morale strong. Sometimes we may feel that we are called to something, yet it doesn't manifest. Many times it happens in a totally different way than we thought, or it takes years before it comes to pass, but just as fruit is sour if picked before it is ripe, so it is with a dream that has not gone through its proper process. "There is a time and a season for everything under the sun."

PRESUMPTION AND FALSE hope are enemies to your well-being. While it is wonderful to be positive and hopeful, it is destructive to get your hopes too high and to presume that things are going to be a certain way. Keep your hopes in check as you take the next step upward toward your prize, but be prepared—you never know when God is going to swoop in and totally change the whole scenario. Yep, embrace it! Change is good!

DAY 84   March 25

WHENEVER WE SEE something good in others, we need to tell them. We all need to hear sweet words, and we can actually change a life with encouraging words. God's Word says, "Pleasant words are like a honeycomb, sweet to the soul and health for the bones." Imagine that your words can actually bring health to others! Why aren't we practicing that more often? If God said, it will work. Let's just do it!

FORGIVENESS IS AGONIZINGLY difficult when someone has hurt you, and long after you have forgiven, the wound lives on in memory. Eventually the wound leaves only a scar that will prove to strengthen your character. When we trust God he will work all things toward good. Your part is to forgive. He does the rest.

DAY 85   March 26

GOD'S WORD SAYS, "I am the Lord that heals you," but this does not mean we can eat and drink and do anything we want and expect our bodies to stay healthy. We live in a very toxic environment. Man has tainted the perfect world that God created, and while we can't avoid every pitfall, it is our responsibility to take care of the vessel we live in. Gluttony in all forms is not only a sin but it's also a killer. God will always do his part, but we have to do our part as well.

LEARNING HOW TO live life is more important than any scholastic education. Even more important than memorizing scripture, it is the application of the Scriptures that really counts. It is not how much we know but how much we do with what we know that counts. "Everything we know is useless if it is not used."

THE INTEGRITY OF the upright will guide them, but the perversity of the unfaithful will destroy them. When we live a good clean life, we will automatically be guided to do what is right, while those who are unsavory and unfaithful to everything in life will destroy themselves. This is not God choosing to hurt people; it is simply the consequences of bad choices that go against the godly principles that were set in place for the good of mankind.

WITH MY GOD I can scale a wall. Life can be overwhelming at times, but if you put things in God's hands and leave them there, he will deliver you from all your fears and bring you into a peaceful, sweet place. Trust him with all your heart. He cares about all the details of your life.

MISTAKES ARE NEVER a total loss, especially if you learn from them. They become almost like a college degree, enabling you to help others and to prevent future errors on your part. A mistake is only harmful if you allow yourself to get bitter. A silver lining lies within every black cloud. Pause and ask God to show you that treasure.

LIFE WITHOUT GOD is like an unsharpened pencil—it has no point. It is empty and hopeless and leaves no need to strive for goodness. All rewards are earthly and temporary. There is nothing more pitiful than a stubborn old buzzard thinking there's nothing good in his life, yet still hanging on to his know-it-all, godless lifestyle. "Seek God while you are still young while you can still find him."

DAY 88   March 29

WHATEVER YOU DO, do it with all your heart. Give everything your best shot. It is so sad to see people trudge their way through life, never really engaging their hearts and then wondering why they are not successful. It does not matter what you do; if you do it well, you will be successful. "Run as if to win the race."

THINGS DO NOT have to be perfect in your life for you to be able to help others. Start where you are and use what you have. Be spontaneous in helping others. When you see a need, and you have the where-withal to help, be that person who lends a helping hand. Your small act of kindness could be the very thing that changes a person's life. Watch for opportunities to be kind to others. "Whatever good thing one man does for another, God will do for him."

DAY 89   March 30

YOU CAN TELL you are a leader if your actions inspire others to dream more, learn more, do more, and become more. Being a leader is wonderful, but it carries with it a huge responsibility. God expects more from leaders. Do not aspire to be a leader unless God has called you, because if you lead people astray, there are consequences to pay.

YOUR OWN STYLE is where you will succeed. While it is "wise to have many counselors," in the end it is your own personal style that will bring you success. It does not matter if no one else in the whole world does things the way you do; your individuality is God-given. Step outside the box of "common." Just as there are no two sets of fingerprints that are the same, so goes the rest of the body. "You are fearfully and wonderfully made" and unique in every aspect.

Day 90   March 31

WE HAVE ALL made dumb decisions, and no matter who we are, we have wondered What was I thinking?! Once you have realized the error and cleaned up the mess, get over it! Don't spend your precious days fretting over it. God says you are forgiven when you ask and that he doesn't even remember it anymore. So pick up the pieces and get on with life!

THE BIBLE TEACHES us that we are blessed not just so we can feel good, not just so we can be happy and comfortable, but so we will bless others. If God can get it through you, he will get it to you. If you live your life only thinking of yourself and being stingy, you will never feel like you have enough. You will always be seeking more. But when you are a giver, there will be a continuous flow of prosperity that comes back to you in every area of life. When we speak of giving, it is not just material things; it is giving of yourself and considering others more important than yourself. It is being "blessed to be a blessing."

April

"GIVE THANKS" IS in the Bible over seventy times. When we say thank you to God, it opens the windows of heaven. The words thank you from a pure, sincere heart are almost magical! A grateful heart will always have favor with both God and man. Never take for granted the things that other people have done to help you along the way. Begin each day with a thankful heart and watch how your life will improve.

MANY TIMES JUST before a great promotion in life we will get hit with all kinds of things that come at us from every direction, trying to convince us that God's plan for our prosperity is not working. It is an unseen force that works in the dark and usually attacks in any area where it has been successful before. It comes to rob, to kill, and to destroy God's creation. But *"God will raise up a standard against this enemy for those who resist the temptation to doubt God and put their trust in him."*

DAY 92   April 2

THERE IS A promise in the Bible that I just love. It says, *"You will be like a tree planted by the water that nothing will shake."* A tree that is planted by the water will always have plenty of water, draught or famine will not affect it, and its leaves will stay green and healthy even as it ages. This is a beautiful visual, and it is promised to those who believe.

BIG DREAMS ARE usually from God. He says he works in us to will and to do his good pleasure, but many of man's dreams are thwarted because of one big enemy, and it's called greed. God will never help you fulfill your dream if greed is at the root. Check your heart for this destructive enemy and ask God to help you as you do your part to fulfill the vision. Work hard, be creative, eradicate greed, acknowledge God, and voila—success!

TRUTH IS NOT simply an academic concept. The way we think about truth has a direct bearing on the way we live our life. There are lots of man-made opinions, but ultimately every truth has come from the Bible. It is the absolute truth and will withstand the test of time. God's Word says, *"Man was created upright, but he devised many schemes."* Concepts come and go. Stick with God's Word and you'll never go wrong.

DON'T JUST SIT around and wait for things to happen. Your blessings are probably going to come from the work of your hands. While God can and does do miracles, most of the time the work of our hands is where the blessings comes from. If you keep moving God will direct your steps, and remember the only thing that can negate the work of your hands is the words of your mouth!"

DAY 94   April 4

SELF-CENTEREDNESS COMES SO easy to mankind, and yet, believe it or not, self-centeredness is one of the main causes of depression, anxiety, sickness, and unhappiness of all sorts. It is not healthy to get inside of yourself and focus on what you feel and your own needs. The world tells you to "take care of number one." But God tells you to *"consider others more important than yourself."* I trust what God says over the world any day of the week. *"Whatever good thing you do for others, God will do for you."*

WE ARE TO move past the fact that people are messed up and in trouble. We are to love them right where they are. It is easy to love the pretty people, but as Christians we are called to love the unlovable, even though sometimes we don't like them. Remember, it is God's loving-kindness working through us that draws them into the kingdom.

DAY 95   April 5

IF WE WANT our lives to change, we have to change our minds first. Change does not happen overnight; it is a process. Do not beat yourself up if you're not where you want to be yet. Set your mind in a place to make changes and enjoy your progress. Our life journey is a journey of process, progress, and change. We have seasons of life that can be dramatically different from the ones before. Be encouraged by the positive progress that you see in yourself no matter how small it may be, and remember, *"God is faithful to finish the work he has started in you."*

YOUR FEELINGS CAN block God's blessings quicker than anything else, and if you don't learn this you'll never walk in God's victory. Feelings are fickle at best. They are one way one day and another way the next day. We are not supposed to live our lives according to how we feel or think. We are supposed to live it by doing what is right. Feelings do not always tell the truth, and what you think is not always correct. Live your life by always doing what is right, no matter how it feels.

DAY 96   April 6

BREAKTHROUGH IS ASSURED if you refuse to give up! Hopes and dreams are much like the birthing process. There is a time of the vision, then the seed planting, next the nurturing and allowing things to form and take shape, and finally the birth itself, with lots of pain and pushing. You have to push through! No backing off. *"Grow not weary of well doing, for in due season you shall have your reward."*

SOMETIMES THE DIFFERENCE between a promotion or staying where you are lies within how you can handle change. It is a waste of time to sit where you are and complain. If you are really unhappy with the situation, be willing to make some changes. Opportunities are everywhere, but you have to be willing to step out of your comfort zone to seize them.

Day 97   April 7

THERE ARE MANY people who think they know it all. They sit in their chairs in their living room and talk back to the TV, believing that they have it all figured out. They are unwilling to budge or even to learn. The Word says, *"Woe to him who is wise in his own eyes."* I don't know about you, but that word *woe* coming from God is very scary. I plan to stay flexible and open all the days of my life. Hope you do too.

ONLY GOD HAS the power to give great wealth, and money is not all there is to great wealth. God chooses to bless those who are willing to share, to be a good steward of what He gives them, and to work with what He gives them. Wealth is a true test of character. God always does what is best for us, and many times, too much money is not best for an individual. Work hard, always do what is right, trust God, and be willing to accept the lot in life that God has provided for you.

DAY 98   April 8

SIN WILL TAKE you will where you don't want to go, keep you there longer than you wanted to stay, and cost you more than you wanted to pay. Sin will eventually cause you to sink to the bottom. You know what's right, and you're just going to have to do it whether you like it or not. God loves you and is always willing to forgive you. *"Life or death, blessing or cursing,"* the choice is yours.

SOME PRAYERS GET answered at FedEx speeds, while others take years. Sometimes it seems that God did not even hear our prayer, and we never see it come to pass. But be assured God hears every prayer and in due season the answer will come, just not always in the way we think. When you feel discouraged, pump yourself up by remembering the times he did answer. Never give up. His plan for you is good. Be expectant, because this could be the day!

DAY 99   April 9

"DO NOT WITHHOLD good from those to whom it is due, when it is in the power of your hand to do so." Our culture has produced a lot of people who seem to be in need, and sometimes it is hard to distinguish between those who are looking for a free handout and those who really need our help. God reminds us in this scripture to be generous. If you have the means and you see a need, you can never go wrong by showing mercy. Even if you're offering is misused, you still get the credit for giving. It is up to each individual to be honest. Do your part right and leave the rest up to God.

BE WILLING TO stand up and fight for the things that are rightfully yours. It is wonderful to be a peaceful person, but do not allow outside influences to steal from you. We cannot always please people. There are times we just have to do what we know is right for ourselves. We should always be kind to others, but we should not allow people to manipulate us. Do what you can and leave the rest to God.

DAY 100   April 10

ENJOY THE RHYTHM of your own life. Everyone's life moves at a different pace. Whining and complaining that you never have any time is a waste of the time that you call so precious. As long as you keep your priorities in order, and keep God at the helm of your ship, a busy life is a blessed life. *"Busy hands and a happy heart."* Enjoy the journey!

WHEN YOU CLING to worthless idols, you are turning away from God, who is the only real deliverance from your mistakes and the problems they have created. An idol is anything that you put above God. We all have little idols in our life: TV, food, football, celebrities, astrology, cars, people—all sorts of things that we have exalted above God. It is not that all these things are bad, they just need to be in their proper place. God should be at the helm of every life.

DAY 101   April 11

GOD LOVES A *"just and balanced weight,"* and this includes balance in every area of your life. While it is important to do your job well, it is important to recharge your batteries. We live in a very hurried world, and sometimes we get so busy sawing that we don't stop to sharpen the saw. Take snippets of time throughout your day or week to refresh yourself. A proverb from the Bible every day has a wonderful way of refreshing.

STUBBORN "RESISTANCE" CAN be a major stumbling block in a friendship or marriage. Always be willing to say, "I am sorry." Stubbornness will harden your heart and block your growth. *Willingness* is the key to overcoming this horrible trait. Be willing to admit your weakness and ask God to help.

THERE IS SUCH power in a made-up mind. As long as we leave an option open, we do not move with the same intensity. Once our mind is made up, we tend to give things our best shot to accomplish our goals. Wavering wastes time and energy, Make up your mind about what you want and go for it!

"I LAY BEFORE you life and death...choose life." God gives us the right to choose, and when we choose to obey the rules that he has ordained for us, the results are a blessed life. When we choose to go against what he says, there will be consequences to pay. When we see others choose a path of destruction, we should pray for them and love them and try to show them a better way, but we should not judge them or try to take away their choice. If God lets them choose, then we need to do the same.

WE CAN ACTUALLY overcome evil with good. Similar to a dark room that one small candle can fill with light, if we as Christians can keep the simplicity of that in mind and allow our light to shine in this dark world, instead of whining and talking about how bad things are, we have the ability to bring light to the world. Yes, it is dark out there, but the light that shines in you can dispel the darkness that is around you, showering light to all who are within your sphere of influence. Don't hide your light under a bushel. And don't allow yourself to blend in with the dark world. "This little light of mine, I'm gonna let it shine! Let it shine, let it shine, let it shine!"

IF WE NEVER step out of our comfort zone, we will eventually find ourselves in a very small box that is boring, mundane, and uninteresting. Variety is truly the spice of life, and it does not take big changes to make this happen. Sometimes simple little changes will make all the difference between a life of drudgery and a life full of adventure and excitement. Try taking a new route to work, get a new hairdo, make something different for dinner, move your furniture. Any little change can make a refreshing difference in your life.

DAY 104   April 14

WE ARE ALL sinners, and God sees all sin as equal. Men tend to separate sin and think that one is worse than another and that someone over there is such a worse sinner. But the truth is every single one of us has issues that are offensive to God. But thank God that he is merciful, and it would behoove all of us to be merciful to others, even those we find repulsive. God loves everyone, and his desire is that all would be saved and come to repentance. We will never win souls to the Lord by judging them. Be kind and play nice.

THERE IS SOMETHING so powerful about saying things out loud. Just thinking something does not activate it like the verbal word does. God tells us that *"the power of life and death are in the tongue"* and if you really want to confirm something you are thinking, verbalize it. He even says that *"faith comes by hearing the word of God,"* which implies that just reading it is not as powerful as reading it out loud. Affirmations work in the same way. Tell yourself what you want to be and act, and your body will follow your words.

DAY 105   April 15

OUR ATTITUDES ARE passed right on down the line, not only to our children, but to everyone we come in contact with. The attitude of one person can affect an entire room of people. A happy person brings joy to everyone, while an old grump troubles everyone around them. Remember, your attitude determines your altitude.

PROVERBS SAYS, *"IF you refuse correction you will go astray."* The know-it-all attitude is dangerous as well as very unbecoming. Always be willing to at least consider a new idea or a different way of doing things. It is so ignorant and unattractive to smugly think you have it all figured out. Stay open and poised to move forward all the days of your life, or you will get left in the dust of antiquity.

YOU MUST REALIZE that accomplishment comes in small increments. Consistent, small steps will result in covering a lot of ground. Don't shoot for the top of the ladder, even though you know that is where you are going, shoot for the next step. This will make your ascent to the top so much easier, and small steps create stability in the final outcome. Line by line, step by step, precept by precept. Keep at it; one day you're there!

BEING HONEST IS not always telling everything that is true. There are a lot of true things that are better left unsaid. Words, even when they are true, can destroy a relationship, discourage people, hurt feelings, and even ruin a life. Everything we say should be true and edifying or it should be kept to yourself. Sticks and stones can break your bones, and words really can hurt you!

DAY 107   April 17

BE DELIBERATE AND diligent in the things that bring security and stability into your life. First and foremost, take care of your spiritual well-being. Anything that is "truth" is actually God's Word, even if the credit for it is not given to God. Seek out these truths and live by them. God will always honor his truths, but be one of the blessed who give him the credit for the beautiful world he has created.

BLESSED IS THE man who remains steadfast under trial. Trials are part of life, and they can actually be a blessing in disguise. Look for the learning curve as you navigate through them and know that each trial that is handled properly brings you closer to God and more successful in life. Every cloud has a silver lining.

DAY 108   April 18

"FORGIVE AND FORGET" is a nice saying but almost impossible to do. While we do have to forgive, we rarely forget. Just like a physical scar that never goes away, an emotional hurt also creates a permanent scar. Allowing your mind to remember over and over what someone did to you is allowing that person to continue to hurt you. It is like continually picking the scab off of a wound and not allowing it to heal. It is okay that you do not forget what happened, but it is not okay to wallow in your pain. What's done is done. Ask God to help you heal, pray for those who have hurt you, and forge ahead.

ADVERSITY BUILDS CHARACTER. The strengthening power of adversity is universally true. Football teams don't win without opposition. Wisdom isn't gained without mistakes, and leaders rarely rise to greatness without crises and tough times. When things go wrong, don't give up. Instead, work through the situation as you keep moving forward, knowing that adversity builds emotional muscle and prepares us for greatness. *"In our weakness, God is shown strong."* Persevere—quitters never win, and winners never quit!

Day 109   April 19

TRUST **IS NOT** a passive state of mind. It is an act of the soul by which we choose to lay hold of the promises of God and cling to them despite adversity. It can be difficult to trust in something that we cannot see, but God's Word says, *"Blessed are those who have never seen but still believe."* Just choosing to believe brings a blessing down on us. Circumstances do not change God's Word, and he tells us many times in the Bible to *"only believe."*

ALL HUMAN EFFORTS are in vain unless they have God's blessing. Sometimes people appear to be successful while they violate God's principles, but the true successful things in life are missing—peace, joy, sweet sleep, patience, true love, good health, and the ability to enjoy what you have. *"Unless God builds the house, it is built on sand!"* Look to God for your blessings, not to the world.

DAY 110   April 20

COMPLAINING NEEDS TO stop! When we complain, we are putting the emphasis on the things that are wrong in our lives instead of focusing on the things that are right. Whatever we dwell on will increase. Keep your focus on the sweet, precious things that are around you. *"If there be anything praiseworthy or noble, think on these things."*

IF FAITH SHOWS up in what you do, you will prove your faith, and faith will bring about miracles. Just saying you have faith is not good enough. You have to put action to your faith. *"Faith without works is dead."* Faith is what makes everything work. Latch on to the hope of living by faith and activate it with positive works.

Day 111   April 21

*"**FAITH IS THE** substance of things hoped for and the evidence of things not yet seen.*" And faith is what activates God's Word. It does not mean that God's Word is not true if you don't have faith, but it does mean that you will probably not see his Word be fulfilled in your life if you do not believe it. Everybody is given an exact measure of faith at birth, but the way we use it is what makes it stronger. It is much like a muscle that if not used will atrophy, but if used will become strong and capable. Faith will only strengthen by hearing God's Word and using it. There is no other way to get this coveted tool that will make or break your life.

WE CAN'T ALWAYS choose what happens to us, but we can choose how we respond to what happens. When we put our trust in God we can rest assured that no matter what happens it will work toward good for us. The peace that comes from knowing that you are in God's hands cannot be bought with anything the world can offer. Tackle one day at a time. Every day has its own set of problems, so concern yourself only with the issues of today, and don't fret over tomorrow.

DAY 112   April 22

EVERYTHING THAT LIVES is either growing or dying. Marriage, friendships, plants, pets—absolutely everything! Some of these things are out of our control, but there is much we can do to bring and maintain life to the things that we have charge over. Love, care, clean, encourage, water, organize, communicate, consider, attend—these are only a few life-giving actions. Be assured that if you are neglecting things, they are dying. If you care, act like it! *"He who tends the tree eats the fruit thereof."*

BLOOM WHERE YOU are planted! The grass is not greener on the other side. Stay put, and cultivate your life. God will move you when you have maxed out where you are. Looking for "greener grass" saps your energy and is a waste of time. Use your energy to enhance where you are.

Day 113   April 23

POSITIVE INPUT FROM the right person at the right time can change lives. We all need to hear positive input, and when we choose to encourage someone, we never know when it can be the difference between success and failure. *"Timely advice is lovely, like golden apples in a silver basket."* A word aptly spoken can be a game changer. Be that person who chooses to give positive input.

EVERY CHOICE WE ever make, good or bad, will make a distinct pattern in the tapestry of our life. God granted us the right to choose, and he tells us to choose life. He has a good plan for our life, but we can actually detour that plan by our choices. Be intentional as you choose the patterns that you want to be woven into this tapestry we call life.

THE FEAR OF God is the beginning of wisdom. It may appear that men are getting by with mocking God and denying his existence, but *"be not deceived, God is not mocked."* We don't have to defend God. He may be patient for a time and let a person paint themselves into a corner, but in the end it is very grievous for those who have denied God. Only a *"foolish man says there is no God."*

GOD'S WORD SAYS that if we try to exalt ourselves, we will get humbled, while if we humble ourselves, we will be exalted. Most people strive to be exalted and think of servitude as demeaning, but God says if we are to become great in his kingdom, we must first become servant to all. Have you been getting knocked down a little lately? Try serving others!

DAY 115   April 25

BE MINDFUL OF the needs around you and remember that when you choose to help the poor, whether spiritually, emotionally, or financially, you are actually doing it as unto the Lord, and there are great rewards. God wants us to enjoy our journey through life, but we should always pay attention to those around us who need our help; the world is full of broken people. Choose to be someone that God can use to help others.

THE POWER OF a made-up mind is amazing! It will carry you through to the end of your dreams. If your mind is made up before the trials and temptations come, you already know exactly how you are going to respond to any given situation, and you will never quit or be thrown off course. God has given us a *"sound, well-disciplined mind."* Operate accordingly!

DAY 116   April 26

PERSEVERANCE IS ACTUALLY more valuable than talent. You can have all the talent in the world, but if you don't have the ability to stick to the program, it means nothing. Potential without perseverance is wasted. There are very few things that won't succeed if you hang in there.

ALWAYS INVOLVE GOD in your plans. Preoccupation with your own plans can actually block God's best in your life and cause you to be stubborn, self-centered, and unable to hear God. While it is important to have a vision, be willing to make adjustments as God fine-tunes your plans. Many times the things you least expect will be the very things that bring you the most joy and success.

LET GO OF your own idea of your identity and trust God to give you an identity that will glorify him and bring you joy. We tend to see ourselves compared to others and of course we compare ourselves to the finest, most beautiful, richest, most popular people. God sees us as unique and individual and we are not in competition with anyone else. Nobody can fill your shoes! God made you special! Ask God to show you how he sees you, and you'll find you have a new spring in your step.

GOD'S WORD SAYS, *"He will never break a bruised reed."* Many times people are bruised reeds due to the traumas of life. If God does not break one of these bruised reeds, we do not have the right to do it either. Harsh, critical rebukes rarely have as profound of an impact as sweet, encouraging words. Plain old love will never fail! *"Those who show mercy will have mercy shown to them."*

DAY 118   April 28

NEVER BELITTLE YOURSELF! And do not carry guilt. Guilt is a heavy load that weighs you down and will keep you from moving forward. If you have asked God to forgive you, God says he doesn't even remember your sin anymore. Your history is not your destiny, and it is a total waste of time to sit around whining about the things you have done wrong. Pick up the pieces and move forward. *"As a man thinks, so he is."* Think kindly about yourself, because what you think is exactly what you will become.

EVEN THOUGH GOD tells us to come boldly into the throne room of God, this does not mean that we are to go in with arrogance or disrespect, demanding that he fulfill his promises. God is omnipotent, and though he is our father, there should always be a deep reverence when we are in his presence. God will always honor his promises. He tells us to ask, but he has a time and a season for all of his plans for us. Ask, believe, and then wait on God.

DAY 119   April 29

IT IS AMAZING what can be accomplished when we don't care who gets the credit. The need to be the big kahuna is a carnal, self-centered trait that we all deal with. Don't allow yourself to enter in. Give credit where credit is due and allow others to shine. God will bless you for that.

YOU WILL NEVER be able to resolve every disagreement. Even though you get along well with someone, there will always be areas where you don't agree. Be kind to the opinions of others but stand your ground on things that you know to be true. This does not mean you should be argumentative. In fact, there are some things that should not be talked about with certain people. The best way to change someone's opinion, especially about God's truths, is to live your life in such a way that they *see* the truth rather than hear it.

DAY 120   April 30

SULKING IS IMMATURE, ungodly, and extremely selfish. Tucking your tail between your legs and running is never the proper way to handle a situation. Although sometimes a quiet time can bring productive thoughts and a calming-down period, the quiet time should not be spent rationalizing why you were right and the other person was wrong. A fair analysis is to admit your part in the problem and make the needed correction from your end. It always takes two to tango. We are called to a life of peace. Do your part to maintain that peace.

GOD'S WORD SAYS, *"I lay before you life and death, choose life."* Choices are our God-given right, and God will always allow us to make choices even when they harm us. God's laws are given for our own good and if they are disobeyed there will always be consequences to pay. Love others, even as you see them making bad choices. Set a good example yourself and *"choose life."*

May

NOTHING CAN BE hidden from God, and *"everything done in the dark will someday come to light."* You may think you got away with something, but in the end everything will be revealed. If you have been wronged by a lie, rest assured that in due season everything will come to the surface. Sometimes it takes years, but I promise, if you let God fight for you, you will come out the victor!

WHEN WE LIE to ourselves, it causes instability. A better choice is to fess up to who you are. Know your strengths as well as your weaknesses, and trust that you can manage your character. You do not have to be stunted by character flaws that have come down from generations before you. Just because you're inclined toward something does not mean you have to live with it; it just means you have to work a little harder in that area. *"God is faithful to finish the work he has started in you."* Do your part and he will do his.

DAY 122   May 2

IF YOU DON'T show mercy to others, God will not show mercy to you, and we desperately need God's mercy. When God doesn't do things your way, it is because he has a better way. If you are believing God for something, trust the process. None of us deserve God's mercy, but he still gives it. Extend that same mercy to others and remember you will only get what you are willing to give.

STRIVING FOR EXCELLENCE is a wonderful character trait, but keep in mind that perfection is just not going to happen while we are on this earth. There are flaws in every single thing and in every single relationship. On the upside, there is also beauty in every single thing and in every single relationship. Whatever is pure, true, noble, right, or lovely, think on these things and give up the nitpicking. It is unproductive and unattractive, and it makes life miserable.

DAY 123 May 3

IF YOU WANT to get over a problem, stop talking about it. Your mouth affects your mind, and your mind sets you in motion. Start talking about positive solutions to negative things. Our mouths have a huge impact on the quality of our lives, and sometimes a "zipped lip" is the best answer.

BEWARE OF NEGATIVE self-talk. Many times our worst enemy is our own thoughts. We think we are not pretty enough, thin enough, rich enough, popular enough, or smart enough. God made you a unique, complete person. You are not patterned after anyone else; you are just you, and no one else has your exact set of talents or abilities. No one else writes, talks, laughs, or does anything else exactly like you. Do not talk negatively about who you are. Take what God gave you and make the most out of it and then give him thanks. This, my friend, is true contentment. *"God knew your name while you were yet in your mother's womb."*

DAY 124   May 4

IF YOU ARE not faithful with the little things in your life, you will not be faithful with anything. No matter what lot in life you find yourself, max it out and take the best possible care of it. If you think your car or your house are old and ugly anyway, you won't bother to keep them clean, and you will never have anything better; you will continue to have an old, ugly house and car. Do the best you can with what you have, and it will increase. This is God's principle, and it works!

DON'T LET LOGIC hinder the pursuit of your dreams. There will always be a logical reason why you should not do something, but success only happens when we push through the obstacles that will almost always be there to detour our success. Ask God for his favor and blessings and then go slay your giants!

DAY 125 May 5

LIVE WITH THE confidence that even if you can't see it, God is still working in your life. Just because you can't see something doesn't mean it is not going on. The old adage "God works in mysterious ways" is absolutely true. Sometimes the very thing that you thought was the devil or a curse turns out to be the thing that God uses to bless you. Just trust God; that is the key.

USUALLY WHEN A leader dies, their popularity will diminish with time. This has not proven true with Jesus. He was crucified and died more than 2,000 years ago, yet today he lives on in the hearts of Christians. There are those who call him teacher, Rabbi, Prophet, or just a good man, but I call him Lord and Savior. His Word is a *"two-edged sword and it will not return void, but will accomplish its intended purpose."* Who is Jesus to you—a liar, or who he says he is? He has to be one or the other. *"As for me and my house, we serve the Lord."*

"BE ANXIOUS FOR nothing, but in all things, with prayer and supplication, make your request be made known to God, and the peace that passes all understanding will guard your heart and your mind through Christ Jesus." I love that promise! God tells us not to be anxious about anything. He gives us explicit instructions in this scripture about how to overcome worry—prayer and supplication. Put the same energy and time toward prayer that you are putting toward worry, and I promise your life will change.

IN OUR SEARCH for security, meaning, peace, and other deep needs in our life, we tend to look "out there" somewhere rather than in the places we are likely to find them. We get attracted to flashy, simplistic solutions and fail to look at the dimmer, often hidden realities that are most times right at our feet and are the average tapestries woven by our own unique set of life circumstances. We look to ourselves and other people, when our real hope lies with God. *"Those who put their trust in God will never be disappointed."*

DAY 127   May 7

WHEN THINGS ARE not working, it is not always necessary to make changes in a broad, sweeping motion. Sometimes small, incremental adjustments will not upset things as much and can still make a huge difference in the outcome of things. Not everything has to be done in a huge, grandiose, dramatic way; most times, just a small tweak will change the whole picture.

WHERE THERE IS no contender, there is no contention. All it takes to resolve any dispute is to step out of the ring. It takes two to tango. Fiery exchanges of words would not happen if there were only one person yapping. Refuse to enter into any kind of combative behavior, and remember that *"the wrath of man can never accomplish the purposes of God."*

DAY 128   May 8

LIFE BECOMES EASIER when you learn to accept an apology you never got. If you can truly forgive and forget, even if the other person was wrong and you were right, you will receive a tremendous reward of peace. And peace is probably the most coveted prize of life. We cannot change the way others will react to things, but we can change our own response. Just forgive! As you forgive, you will be forgiven.

YOU CAN'T DO everything you want to do in life. You have to make your choices and be happy with them. We all have thoughts of "the path not taken." But don't allow yourself to get caught up in, or long for, those unfulfilled dreams. Move on with your life choices, maximizing all the little details as you accept and take pride in what is yours. When you are faithful with what you have, God will always give you more."

DAY 129   May 9

WHEN WE SERVE God, things can appear to be falling apart, when they are actually falling into place. Just because something did not go as you thought does not mean it is finished. It means God has another plan! Flow with it, trusting God as you go.

SOMETIMES WE GET into intense relationships with people we don't even like, but interestingly we are not called to like people, but to love them. In fact, we are *commanded* to love them, and God never gives us a command that includes emotions or is impossible. This kind of love is a choice. While it is easy to love the unlovable from a distance, it can be daunting to love them up close. Blessings always ensue when we choose to follow this command that is actually the whole crux of Christianity. You don't have to like them; just love them!

DIRTY, TIRED, SLOPPY, unenthused, uneducated, out of shape, lazy, stubborn, grumpy, bad attitude, always late, unreliable—it all matters. It is not luck that causes a life to be successful; rather, it is the continuous flow of all the little things in life that matter. It is taking charge of your life and recognizing your weak areas and making the needed corrections. It is doing everything you do in an excellent way. It is the way your countenance looks, it is the way you dress and conduct yourself. Ask God to help you and then set your mind to succeed.

GOD PROMISES THAT he will *"lead us along unfamiliar paths, turn darkness into light, and make the rough places smooth."* I don't know about you, but that scripture just delights me. Imagine the creativity in life that God will give to those who look to him to honor his promises. God will never force himself on you, but when you are ready, ask him for help. *"He draws close to those who draw close to him."*

Day 131   May 11

THE TRUE RICHES of life are not represented by money. A far greater blessing is the ability to appreciate what you have. You can have all the money in the world, but if you don't have the gift of appreciation, you don't have anything. With this sweet gift you will find contentment, and love what is yours—whether you have little or much. You will see those things that are yours as beautiful and not covet what belongs to others. And that, my friends, represents true wealth.

ENJOY YOUR RELATIONSHIP with yourself. If you do not like yourself, it will be hard for others to like you. The Word says to *"love others as you love yourself."* And you are actually not even capable of loving others if you cannot love yourself. Don't focus on your failures or your shortcomings. Do the best you can with what you have, forgive yourself, and trust that *"God is faithful to finish the work he has started in you."*

DAY 132   May 12

WE ARE FREE from our past. Nothing you did in your past could cut you off from the love of God. The key is to really let it go and forget it. The past should not be looked at any more than your rearview mirror. Keep your eyes on the windshield and only glance in the rearview mirror occasionally for safety purposes. Living in the past will rob you of the here and now, and your future. *"Forgetting those things that are behind and looking forward to those things that are ahead."*

SUCCESS IS NOT based on IQ, talent, potential, or any other coveted attribute. It is simply based on plain old GRIT! *Grit* is perseverance and passion toward a long-term goal, coupled with determination and continuity. It is not a "lucky break," it is just plugging away and pushing forward through the maze of trials that life presents. It is getting backup when you are knocked down, it is a commendable work ethic, and most important of all, it is fueled by the promise that says, *"I can do all things through Christ who strengthens me."*

WE DON'T ALWAYS know why our heart is leading us in a certain way, but if it is right, then just do it. God promises to direct the steps of the righteous so trust that He is directing you, and even if it appears you have made some wrong choices, he will work all things toward good. Be confident that God is directing you and just move toward your heart.

THE BIG LIE is that you can do anything you want in life. You will never be anything but mediocre until you learn to play into your own strengths. We all have strengths, and this is where you should put your energy. Competing with others and trying to be like them will never allow you to operate optimally. It is good to glean from others, but ultimately be who God created you to be.

DAY 134   May 14

EVERY ACT OF love will set you free, especially if it is not expected or deserved. It is easy to show love to the lovable, but the huge blessing comes when you go over and above. If you can rise above your situation and do the unexpected, you will find a blessing there that will make you feel so good. Don't allow yourself to enter in to the selfishness that is rampant in our world today; instead, show another way. *"Love never fails."*

IT'S MUCH EASIER to make a decision and work into the feelings than to let your feelings make the decisions. Feelings will come and go, but decisions are made. Decisions should always be made based on what is right, not on what you feel. Our flesh is weak, selfish, greedy, and indulgent and it should never be allowed to control us. It doesn't matter if you don't want to do what is right; do it anyway. Make that decision ahead of time.

Day 135   May 15

IF YOU THINK too much, you will create problems in your head that aren't even there. While it is not good to just skim the surface of life, it is not good to be too intense either. Granted, there are times that deep thinking can produce a brilliant idea, but it is usually healthier to keep your hands moving. Don't worry about tomorrow, for it will have its own worries; instead, consider the task at hand, remembering that you are blessed according to the work of your hands.

WHEN WE ASKED God for help, most of the time he leads us and shows us how to help ourselves. We cannot just sit idly by and expect the blessing to fall out of the sky. We are often involved in the answer to our own prayers. God's Word says, *"We are blessed according to the work of our hands."* If you do not know what else to do, just keep your hands moving and God will direct.

Day 136   May 16

"BUT THE PATH of the just is like the shining sun, that shines ever brighter unto the perfect day." Don't you just love that promise?! Boy, I sure do. Those words conjure up a beautiful visual of life getting sweeter and sweeter as the years go by. So who are the "just" that are referred to? *"Those who walk blamelessly, do what is right, do not slander, and honor and fear the Lord."* These promises are for those who claim the Lord as their Father, much like a will that a parent leaves to her children. This is the promise to those who serve God."

PRIDE CAUSES DISTORTION, deception, and blindness It has to puff itself up and lie to stay afloat, and it refuses to see the truth or admit when it is wrong. It is not teachable, and is jealous and competitive with others—very destructive behavior. It comes before a fall. Blessings follow humility.

DAY 137   May 17

WHEN GOD IS your hiding place he will preserve you from trouble. God has actually provided a hiding place that is available to those who trust him. Realistically, there can still be havoc and chaos swirling around us, but that hiding place will be a divine place of ultimate protection no matter what the circumstances look like—a promise that all things will work toward good; a promise that no matter what happens, God has your back. *"This is the heritage of those who serve the Lord."*

WHENEVER YOU SUFFER a loss in which you are either a victim or faultless, God will always replace it for you. Sometimes he says if it is a rip-off you will receive seven times over what you lost. Be encouraged; in the end justice will always be done. If the loss was your own doing, and you repent, it will also be restored after the consequences have run their course.

Day 138   May 18

"WITH WHATEVER MEASURE you use, it will be measured back to you." We often use this scripture when we are talking about giving money or stuff. But God never says one thing at a time; this scripture refers to everything in life. Whatever you put out there, and with whatever quantity you put it out there, it will come back on you. The good, the bad, and the ugly! We do not get by with anything. *"Do unto others as you would have them do unto you."* You get to choose your own blessing or cursing. Choose well.

PROVERBS SAYS, "THERE *is one who makes himself rich yet has nothing, and one who is poor but is rich."* Money and "stuff" can be so much fun, but it can also bring much sorrow. If riches are ill gotten in any way, they are not a blessing and will create all sorts of havoc in one's life. Material riches are not what make one rich. *"Faith, hope, and love"*—these are the true riches of life. If you have "faith" for, "hope" to latch on to, and you are surrounded by "love," then you are rich! Bathe yourself in these three glorious gifts, and all other things will be added.

Day 139   May 19

HAPPINESS IS SOMETHING you decide on ahead of time. If you make a decision that you are going to be grateful and happy with whatever life presents, and you don't nitpick your way through life, noticing all the flaws, and if you don't set your expectations too high, and you choose to see the beauty in everything, life can truly be a bowl of cherries! I choose to be happy. How 'bout you?

IT DOESN'T TAKE big things to please people. Most of the time small, simple acts of kindness will go a long way. One rose or even a hand-picked wildflower means as much as a whole bouquet when given with a loving spirit. Don't put off doing something sweet for someone just because you think you don't have enough money or enough time or you want to wait until you can do something grandiose. Just do something simple and from your heart, and watch the results.

Day 140   May 20

GOD TELLS US to *"be strong and courageous."* Courage does not mean you don't have fear. Courage is doing something in spite of fear! Courage is stepping out and doing what needs to be done regardless of what you may feel. It is going the extra mile or navigating where others are afraid to go. Courage is sticking your head above the crowd and attempting something new; it is always proactive rather than reactive. Courage is fully trusting God and expecting a miracle even in the face of hopelessness. *"Be strong and courageous."*

THERE ARE TIMES you win and yet lose, and there are times you lose and yet win. Winning is not always the best for us, and losing is not always detrimental. Losing can be one of the best teachers. Remember, God always works everything toward good for believers—even a loss. The iron that's been through the fire is the strongest.

NEVER DO OR say anything that a simple apology will not take care of. One careless remark or action can set your life on a course of destruction. Your tongue is a powerful weapon and can be used to bless your life or curse your life. Make an out-loud proclamation that you will take charge of every word that comes out of your mouth! If you don't control your tongue, it will control you.

WHEN YOU LEAD (and everyone is a leader at some point), intentionally lead with the humility of wisdom, and be a servant as you lead. A true godly leader is not a pompous know-it-all but, like Jesus, is willing to wash the feet of his students. That is true servant leadership.

WHEN A PERSON feels appreciated, they will always do more than expected. If you want your children, your husband/wife, or your employees to improve, try using words of encouragement. It is a natural instinct that is built into man to want to live up to the good that is said or thought of them. *"A word fitly spoken is like apples of gold in settings of silver."* While negative words have the opposite impact. Remember, *"the power of life and death are in the tongue."* Speak with positivity and intentionality. *"The tongue of the wise brings healing."*

WE HAVE ALL done or said things in the past that we wish we would not have done, and we will probably do things in the future that we should not do. This does not make you a bad person and does not define who you are. As long as you recognize your errors, you are forgiven. God says that if you have asked for forgiveness, he does not even remember your sin. So if God is so willing to forgive your sins, why are you remembering them? Simply make restitution where you can and leave the rest to God. Get on with life!

DAY 143   May 23

GUILT GRIEF IS the worst kind of grief. We are all going to deal with losing a loved one at some time in our lives, and if you can go through the loss without guilt it is so much easier. Comfort yourself with the fact that regrets are a part of every relationship, but don't allow guilt to prevail. Refuse to entertain this tormentor. Make restitution when you can and give the rest to God. He never uses guilt to punish his children.

GRUDGES ARE LIKE body weight. They weigh us down and cause us to feel sluggish and cumbersome, and just as body weight is dangerous for our health, so is the weight of a grudge. *"It is foolish to carry a grudge."* Most of the time a grudge has a need to get even, and God says that he is the judge, not you. Relieve yourself of the weight of carrying a grudge. Take the offender off of your hook and put him on God's hook. God will always see that justice is done. *"He loves a just and balanced scale."* Trust him.

PRAISING AND THANKING God will keep your faith strong and keep oppression and depression away from you. Gratefulness is crucial to staying happy. Instead of grumping and griping, try looking for something good about even the most trying situation, and thank God for it. This will always lift your spirits no matter what is going on, and will give this positive courtesy to those around you as well. A positive outlook causes everyone to work at their peak capacity.

CLINGING TO YOUR personal deficits in life will only strengthen them. There is nothing wrong with admitting that you were wrong or that you have a weakness in a given area (we all have them), but what is wrong is to deny them or hold them close. It is not a weakness to admit you are wrong; it is a strength. God is faithful to finish the work he has started in you, but you have to do your part to continue to evolve into a better person. Never stop growing, changing, and learning no matter how old you get.

DAY 145 May 25

WHEN YOU SLING mud, you will get mud on yourself. Choose to take the high road even when others are raging. We do not elevate ourselves by putting others down; in fact, what you say about others will come back on you like a boomerang. *"As you do unto others, it will be done unto you."* Play nice!

WHAT'S DONE IS done. It is unproductive and depressing to sit around and think about things that cannot be changed. Once the eggs are scrambled, there is no way to unscramble them. Work with what you have. Don't sit around wishing the eggs were not scrambled, because they are. Mistakes happen. Be kind to the human frailties of yourself and of others. Forgive, and move on with a determination to learn from mistakes.

DAY 146   May 26

THERE IS A great temptation to measure oneself by the standards of others; it is an effort in futility and cannot have any positive outcome. God tells us not to compare ourselves one to the other because it will always either make us vain or cause us to feel inadequate. We are all individually and wonderfully made, none exactly alike. Experience and appreciate the uniqueness of yourself as well as of others.

PUTTING OTHERS DOWN will never make you look better; in fact, it makes you look really ugly. Women especially tend to think that by putting other women down, it takes them out of the competition. Not true! I think all of us have participated in this ugly character trait at one time or another, and we all need to stop it. Poking fun or degrading, even in supposed jest, is not nice. Appreciate everyone's unique character, including your own. *"Consider others more important than yourself."*

DAY 147   May 27

GOD USUALLY LEADS you with whispers rather than screams. You will hear a voice behind you say, *Stop, go this way.* It is not an audible voice (although it could be). It is a gentle urging within your spirit that is always pure and peaceful. Usually you will feel confirmation in your own heart that this is right. Many times God uses people to confirm what you've already heard; if you hear it two or three times, listen up!

WHEN YOU FEEL you are giving sacrificially or like others have taken advantage of your generosity, keep in mind God's promise that *"with whatever measure you measure out, it will be measured back to you."* Do not look to man to reward you, even though God will often use others, but ultimately it is God who rewards. If you keep your heart right when giving, your reward will always be greater than your sacrifice. *"When you give, it will be given back to you, pressed down, shaken together, and running over."*

DAY 148   May 28

THE CHOICES YOU make today have a huge impact on your future. Every wrong choice takes you farther away from your heart's desire. Ask God daily to direct your steps and then stay on the lighted path he lays before you.

LET BYGONES BE bygones. Whining over the past and thinking about what you could have done, or should have done, is a waste of time and energy. What you did or did not do is a fact of life, and now you have to deal with the consequences of your choices and try to learn from your mistakes. Mistakes are a part of life and they can actually be wonderful learning tools. The wise man learns from his mistakes, while the fool does the same things over and over and expects the outcome to be different.

DAY 149   May 29

MANY TIMES WHAT seems like a negative turn of events in your life might actually be a part of God's plan for you. Choose to be grateful whether you have little or much. Some prayers are just not answered and we don't know why, but God has a plan. Trust and believe, and never give up hope. Remember that faith needs hope to latch on to, and faith is what activates God's Word in your life.

THINGS HAPPEN TO us every day from minor to major that could serve as an excuse for vengeance, and each time something hurtful happens we have a choice to make. Will we be peacemakers or revenge seekers? Peacemakers bring blessings on themselves and others. Revenge seekers bring curses and strife. *"The noblest revenge is to forgive."*

DAY 150 May 30

DECEPTION ALWAYS FOLLOWS pride, because pride has a need to be handsome. It needs to appear strong, rich, smart, confident, and always needs to be right. It will have to deceive to prove its point. Pride is a bondage that keeps the real you bound up. Transparency is so liberating!

WHEN WE LOOK at a situation in our life, we only see the moment, and oftentimes the situation from our perspective looks hopeless. But God sees the whole picture. The road of life is paved with lots of twists and turns and many potholes, but if you keep your eyes on God and on the prize that awaits all of us who serve him, he promises that he will walk through this life with us and that *even if we stumble the angels will hold us up.* Be strong and courageous!

Day 151   May 31

THE WORLD'S PEACE can disappear very quickly. The world can give peace, but takes it away. God gives us a legacy of lasting peace. The peace of the believer is deep, calm, and everlasting, *"the peace that goes beyond understanding."* The world, with all its blandishments, cannot give it, and the world, with all its fluctuations, cannot take it away.

IT IS ONLY the fear of God that can deliver us from the fear of man. As you learn to trust and fear our awesome God, you will be delivered from fear. Remember the Word says, *"Perfect love casts out all fear."* So the opposite of love is not hate, it is fear. If you are dealing with fear of any kind, it is only because you have not learned to truly trust God. It doesn't mean you don't believe in him, it just means you do not know him very well. He is knocking at your door. Get to know him by reading his Word and praying.

June

EMBRACE CONTENTMENT! LIFE is never perfect, and if we are always expecting perfection in ourselves, our loved ones, and our surroundings, we will always be discontent. A better choice is to see things through grateful eyes, as you fix and change those things that are within your control and leave the rest to God. I actually love the Pollyanna outlook that believes and acts like *"all things work together for good." "As you believe, it is done unto you." "Only believe."*

MANY PEOPLE OWE the grandeur of their life to great difficulties. Ask God to show you the learning curve that is there in every situation. Make an intentional decision to come out of every trial better rather than bitter. It's your choice!

DAY 153   June 2

HUMAN NATURE TENDS to get negative in the difficult times, but God tells us to count it all joy when we fall into trials. On the other side of every setback and every test is a new opportunity. Don't miss the blessing by focusing on the negative. There is a blessing in every valley. Make up your mind to enjoy life and to be happy regardless of your circumstances. *"In all things give thanks."*

MANY TRIALS WILL come in our lifetime, and many of them will be overwhelming. But God's Word says that if you remain steadfast during these trials, *"you will be blessed."* The old adage "Every cloud has a silver lining" is true. Weather your storms with a complete trust in God, and blessings will follow.

DAY 154   June 3

GOD NEVER USES guilt to punish us. Guilt will take you down if you let yourself wallow in it. God's Word says that if we have asked for forgiveness, God does not even remember our sin anymore. This does not mean that there are not consequences to the things that we do wrong. The antidote for guilt should be to ask God and others for forgiveness, receive the forgiveness, and then be patient as you work through the consequences that are part of the process. I personally always ask God to be gentle with me as he teaches me.

THERE MAY NOT be a trumpet sound or loud applause when we make a right decision, just a calm sense of resolution and peace. Right decisions are paramount for a happy life. God built a natural sense of right and wrong into all of us. Listen for that still, quiet voice that comes from within, and proceed accordingly.

DAY 155   June 4

THE LORD SPECIALIZES in using people with small numbers, meager resources, and insufficient strength. If you feel disappointed today because of some small statistic in your life, remember that he tells us, *"Do not despise small beginnings."* The real value of something is amassed little by little. The Word says that *"money quickly gotten is quickly lost."* It is better to be faithful and to continue with your small numbers, knowing that you are gaining strength as you grow. This is true whether it be emotional, physical, financial, or relational. Little by little...one brick at a time... faithful. You shall have your reward.

PSALM 91 SAYS, *"He shall cover you with his feathers, and under his wings you shall take refuge."* God's protection of his children is likened to a mother hen with all of her baby chicks safely tucked under her wings. God has provided this kind of covering for us. Lean on this picture when you are struggling with life. As long as you are honestly seeking to walk the path that God has provided for you, this scripture is yours. Believe it and trust it and when the going gets tough, snuggle in close to your Father in heaven; he will always be there for you.

DAY 156   June 5

THE LUSTS OF the flesh war against your soul. If you allow your flesh to rule, you will eat and drink too much, you will not exercise, you'll be greedy, jealous, competitive to a fault, you will participate in all sorts of sexual disorders, and you could even kill someone. The flesh is warring against the things of the Spirit. The Word says, *"The flesh is weak but the spirit is strong."* Take charge of your flesh or it will take charge of you.

DON'T DESPISE SMALL beginnings, because everything in life that is amassed little by little has great value. If you keep plugging away at something and you do your best as you go, in the end it will gain momentum like a snowball. When you get things quickly, it usually doesn't last. Be faithful, diligent, and patient with what God has given you to do. Set your hand and your mind to it and watch it prosper.

DAY 157   June 6

SPEAK THE TRUTH in love and with tact, or keep your mouth shut. People who boast that they just "tell it like it is" and allow things to shoot out of their mouth without any thought of how it will make others feel are rude and ignorant. While honesty is a beautiful trait, it should never be shared in a way that hurts the feelings of others. Honesty coupled with love and tenderness is of great value. *"Gracious words are like a honeycomb, sweet to the soul and healing to the flesh."*

NOT ALL ANGER is wrong. There is such a thing as righteous anger, and I believe that one of the biggest problems in our world today is apathy—a refusal to get involved. It is selfish and slothful to stand by and allow suffering of any kind on the pretext of "It's none of my business." Be cognizant of the wrongs that are done within your realm of influence and do what you can when you can. God says to *"fight for those who cannot fight for themselves."*

DAY 158   June 7

THERE IS ALWAYS an option to quit in every situation, but there are some things in life that this option should not be left on the table. As long as we know we could quit, we never quite do as good of a job. The moment we remove "the quit option" from any situation, we actually have the victory. Pinpoint these important areas in your life and make a decision today that you are never going to quit. "Winners never quit and quitters never win."

STAY BALANCED BETWEEN reality and the spirit realm. Sometimes we get so caught up in the spirit realm that we forget about reality. We are in the real world and we have to live here peacefully. At the same time, the world tends to forget that there is a very real spirit world. While we *wrestle not against flesh and blood,"* it is still important to include the arm of the flesh. I believe the combination of bringing these two important worlds together in our life is the difference between success and failure."

DAY 159 June 8

BE CAREFUL ABOUT comparing your life to that of someone else or with the way things used to be. It is also harmful to compare your life with fantasies that bear little resemblance to reality. Make every effort to accept and appreciate your lot in life, while looking for good to emerge from even the worst situations. Learning to be content is both a discipline and an art. Train your mind to trust God's sovereign ways with your life.

BE WILLING TO yield to others. Stubborn know-it-alls will end up painting themselves into a lonely, boring, no-growth corner. We all have things to learn from each other. Never allow yourself to get to the place that you think you know it all, because the Word says, *"Be careful when you think you stand lest you fall."* Stubbornness brings all sorts of ugly things into your life.

Day 160   June 9

WE STAND ON level ground in the realm of God's mercy. He loves everyone the same, but what we do with God's mercy for us can change the destiny of those around us, and particularly for our families. *"The rain falls on the just and the unjust at the same time."* If you are associated with those who are blessed, the blessing will fall on you as well. Choose your friends accordingly.

THERE'S A DEPTH of sorrow, pain, anger, disgust, or any negative reaction that you should never let yourself go to. While it is okay and sometimes even necessary to release pain and anger and other negative feelings, keep a handle on your emotions. There is a depth that is hard or even impossible to overcome, and the energy it saps from you can be devastating. Always keep charge of your flesh. It is weak, but your spirit is strong. Let it reign!

DAY 161 June 10

GOD'S WAYS ARE higher than our ways, and sometimes something that seems bad is really just God working something out in our life. When we don't understand God, we tend to resist the things we perceive as bad and it wears us out. Remind yourself that just because something feels bad, it isn't necessarily bad for you. Learn to trust God even when your circumstances are hard to understand.

FIGHT FOR YOUR life! Don't curl up in a ball or roll over; get up and start swinging! God will fight for you, but I believe that sometimes he uses our own willingness to stand up and take charge. Speak verbally to those things in your life that you want to go. Open a door in your house and tell depression, poverty, anger, and anything else that is troubling you to be gone in the name of Jesus, and then do not let it back in. Everything must bow to the name of Jesus!

DAY 162   June 11

RELIGIOUS MAGIC WILL not work. If you are not serving God, do not expect him to bail you out. What is your purpose for praying? Are you using God, or are you serving God? Quit thinking he is just useful. Gimmicks won't work. Honor and serve him. That works!

WHEN WE ENCOURAGE others, it causes them to flourish. It is like putting fertilizer on plants. We should never withhold encouragement when it has such a positive effect on others. There is always something nice that we can find to say. If everyone would operate in this sweet gift, the world would be a much better place. Do your part. Encourage someone today.

DAY 163   June 12

STRIVE TO BECOME the most authentic, true version of yourself possible. While it is good to glean from one another, remember that you are special and unique. Strive to be the incredible person that God has created you to be. Max out and manage your own character. We all have tweaks; acknowledge and take responsibility for them. Work on making the needed corrections in the flaws that you find. If you don't learn to love yourself, you will have difficulty loving others.

YOU WILL NEVER get more out of something than you are willing to put into it. It is simple math. You can't plant corn and expect to harvest watermelon. You can't fill your piggy bank with pennies and expect hundred-dollar bills to appear. We may wish magical results, but the cause-and-effect principle will still remain. *"As a man sows, so shall he reap."* This principle will prove true in absolutely every aspect of your life. If you want to win in life, *"run your race as if to win."*

DAY 164   June 13

WE CAN EASILY drop back into the condemnation that a tarnished past can bring to mind. A picture, a song, a word, or one small insinuation of the grievance can fire up the memory of things better forgotten. Refuse to receive condemnation. If Jesus is your Lord and if you have asked for forgiveness, *"it is done!"*

GOD MAKES A promise to those who love him and keep his commandments that his covenant will never be broken to them—that they can count on his word. *"Has he said it, and will he not do it?"* Your doubt about God and his word does not change God or what he says, but what it does change is your ability to receive those wonderful gifts! God has given amazing, comforting, magical promises, and I find it foolish to reject them. It is everyone's individual free choice, but I tell you this: I claim those promises for me and my household and thank God for his mercy, grace, and generosity.

DAY 165   June 14

THE WORD SAYS, *"God will give power to the weak."* People who think they don't need God and think they are strong will have to go it alone. Until you reach a point in your life that you realize you are weak and cannot make it without God's help, God will never interfere with your choices. I have heard people say that religion is a crutch for weak people. This is absolutely the truth, but it is also true that we are all weak; the sooner a person realizes that, the sooner they can begin their majestic journey through life.

BE CAREFUL ABOUT making assumptions based on limited information. Those assumptions could lead you down a path with a dubious outcome. You will eventually have to retrace your steps to get back on solid ground. In the meantime, you will have a difficult time knowing the difference between what is true and what is false. If you find yourself in this shadowy place, be willing to face the possibility that you could be wrong and always be willing to at least listen to an opposing opinion. When all else fails, Google it! Information is right at your fingertips; check before you blab your mouth. *"The words of the wise are as sturdy as well-driven nails."*

ONCE YOU HAVE asked God for wisdom, trust that you have it. Do not doubt that you received it. God tells us if we ask for wisdom he will give it to us liberally. It is okay to get confirmation from other people, but do not allow people to change the wisdom that God has given you. When listening to others speaking into your life, be sure that you have a witness in your own spirit before proceeding with anything they may recommend. God does use people, but be careful that you don't put their ideas ahead of what God has given you. You will know in your gut what God wants for you.

I HAVE HEARD it said that Jesus is a crutch for weak people. This is absolutely true! There are times in everyone's life that we feel bulletproof and can handle everything, but then those things hit that come out of nowhere—that we have no control over—and we really, really need a crutch. Every single one of us needs a crutch! The foolish man says "there is no God" and chooses to limp through life alone, beating his chest pridefully.

DAY 167   June 16

THERE'S NOTHING SWEETER than two people who choose to consider each other more important than themselves. This is what makes a made-in-heaven marriage or friendship. We all have tweaks and annoying little habits. "Be to their virtues very kind; be to their faults a little blind."

LEGALISM STOPS PEOPLE from enjoying life. Legalism nitpicks and tries to find what people do wrong. It puffs itself up and thinks it is better than everyone else. Even though legalistic people may claim to be godly and can usually quote scripture, they are not operating the way Jesus told us to operate. He said, *"You will know them because they love each other."* Legalists really just love themselves rather than others. Beware and steer clear.

DAY 168   June 17

WE ARE FEARFULLY and wonderfully made. When we consider how intricate and how beautifully our bodies operate, it is absolutely inconceivable to believe that we could evolve from a piece of slime. I personally believe that atheism is "ignorance gone to seed." I believe that an atheist chooses not to believe because they do not want to be accountable to God or anyone else, but in the end there will be a time of judgment and everyone will stand before the Almighty, including atheists. Not a pretty thought."

TRIALS DO NOT define who you are, but they do determine who you become. Sometimes there are things that you just cannot figure out and that you are going to have to handle the best way you can. God tells us not to lean on our own understanding, yet we waste so much valuable time overanalyzing why this or that happened when, in truth, most of the time we will never be able to figure it out, nor do we need to. Clean it up the best you can and trust that God will do the rest, then get on with life!

DAY 169   June 18

YOU ARE THE sum total of your opportunities and choices in life, and it would be good for you to review the past briefly to understand more completely where you are now and how you got here. There are adjustments to be made at this juncture, and the more understanding you have, the better able you are to have sound judgment and to make good choices in your future. *"Be wise as a serpent and gentle as a lamb."*

THERE ARE SEASONS in life when it will be difficult to praise God. But be determined that you will praise him no matter what you see with your eyes or what your circumstances may look like. There is a scripture that says, *"Praise for the spirit of heaviness."* So praising God will actually lift depression and heaviness off you. If we want God's promises to work in our life, we have to do it the way he says. If God tells us to turn right and we turn left because we want to do things our way, we are not going to make it to the Promised Land. We get to choose.

WHEN WE CHOOSE to do the right thing, it shows more love than all the words in the world. Love should be played out as a verb; it requires action to be effective. Being trustworthy in all your choices will solidify your ability to love and be loved. It brings favor with man and God.

WORRIED OR STRESSED? One secret to healthy life-long relationships and success is a good response to bad news. Face problems joyfully because problems are inevitable, and how you handle them will largely determine the outcome. It is not always easy to be joyful in negative situations, but it is also said that it takes less energy to smile than to frown. Make a determined decision that you are going to be known as someone who is part of the solution rather than part of the problem. Comfort yourself and others in the throes of a problem with this wonderful promise: *"Weeping may endure for a night, but joy comes in the morning."*

SOMETIME IN LIFE you will have to take a leap of faith. Look to God for encouragement and then JUMP! If you do not jump, you will always be mediocre at best. Everything that is worth anything in life requires a jump at some point, and playing it safe will never produce a big harvest. Not every jump is smooth sailing, but it will always propel you forward and position you for your grand finale. I am a huge believer in "no guts, no glory," and when you trust God, *guts* is nothing more than faith.

DOUBT WILL HINDER your prayers. Remember, *"as you believe, it is done unto you."* When you have prayed, *"believe you have received."* When you don't believe, it doesn't change God's Word but it will change how it affects your life. Make a choice to believe God's Word even if it doesn't make sense to you. You do not have to understand God's Word to have it work in your life. God makes it so easy! He says, *"Only believe."*

Day 172   June 21

PONDER THE PATH you are on in your life and consider where it is leading. We need to establish our direction and not just wander around hoping to bumble into the Promised Land. Set goals and have a plan. Even though God may change your direction, it is still important that you have a vision as you go; just keep moving and he will direct your path just as he promised.

WE SHOULD ALL be striving for excellence rather than perfection. The definition of *excellence* is "unusually good, and surpasses ordinary standards." Perfection is unattainable; it is flawless, and striving to reach it can cause disappointment and even torment. Relax and enjoy life as you do your absolute best and seek to be excellent at all you do. What is excellent within your realm of capabilities is all that God expects of you.

DAY 173   June 22

WE ARE CALLED to faithfulness rather than to greatness, and many of our good works will not only go unnoticed but can even appear to turn on us. However, *"Be not deceived. As a man sows, so shall he reap."* Just as perverse choices will eventually turn on you, good, fair, ethical, kind choices will eventually pay off as well. No matter how things may appear, *"grow not weary of well doing because in due season you shall have your reward."* That's a promise!

DO NOT BECOME a victim of regret. Like shame, regret is a waste of time, and God never uses shame or regret to correct his children. God uses conviction, which is a gentle urging when we are doing something that does not please him, or will harm us. Conviction does not bring about grief, shame, or anxiety. Once you have done what you can do to make restitution for errors in life, turn the page and get over it.

DAY 174   June 23

GOD TELLS US to *"bring him in remembrance of his word."* I remind him of his promises when I make my requests in prayer. This assures me that I have done my part and the rest is up to him. Unfortunately, most people never take the time to read the Bible, so they don't even know what the promises are. Don't be one of those people. Read your book of instructions. Everything just works better when life is done the way the manufacturer intended.

OUR PERSPECTIVE ON life is based on how we choose to see it. Everyone struggles with something in life. We can set about solving the problems and allowing the experience to make us better, or we can wallow in our self-pity and become bitter. It's always a choice.

DAY 175   June 24

STUBBORNNESS IS AN ugly character trait that will prevent us from progressing and learning new things. It will cause us to box ourselves in, and life will become very mundane and boring with very little variety. Life is more fun if we are willing to open up and try new things. It is pitiful to see old people who are stuck in the past and not willing to go forward. Life is a collage of movement and change. Experience every moment of it, right to the end of your life. There are new hidden treasures everywhere. Watch for them!

WHEN YOU KNOW that God really loves you, it makes you look bold and brave. When you really know that God is for you, and that no one can be against you if God is on your side, it gives you the confidence to go out in the world and find success. God loves all of us, but unfortunately many people do not know that or accept it as a reality in their life. He's holding his hand out to you; just take it.

DAY 176 June 25

HAPPINESS DOES NOT start with your friends, your job, or your bank account. It starts with you. Wake up each day and determine in your heart to be happy! Life is full of challenges and always will be. Ask God for help and confront them one at a time. Got a lemon? Make lemonade!

UNFORGIVENESS IS UNFORGIVENESS, and will block your blessings and cripple your ability to love others, even unforgiveness toward yourself. In fact, I think holding aught against yourself is the worst, because you will only love others as much as you love yourself. Unforgiveness is an acid that will literally eat you alive. You have to make the choice to forgive and once you have done that, ask God to help you apply that forgiveness. *"Ask and you shall receive."*

TOUCH CAN BE so healing. It is so simple to touch someone in a loving way and it can mean so much to them. The Word says, *"If a believer lays hands on the sick, they shall recover."* Imagine just touching someone who is sick and having them get well. Be quick to lovingly touch others, knowing that it has powerful ramifications for the receiver. Touch is an awesome language in itself; sometimes words are not even necessary. Touch can independently portray love.

THE WORLD IS full of noncommittal people. God's Word says, *"Let your yea be yea and your nay be nay."* Without solid commitments, marriage and friendships suffer, as does the one who refuses to make or keep them. Not making commitments is nothing more than wavering, and God's Word says, *"Those who waver get nothing from him."* Make a commitment today to operate in this ethical attribute.

Day 178   June 27

IF WE CHOOSE to cheat others, even if it is a little tiny cheat, we open ourselves up to all kinds of curses. We absolutely do not get by with anything. We may think we pulled one off, but be assured it will come back on you. If you want a good life, always choose to do what is right. Treat others as you want them to treat you, because your treatment of others is exactly what you will get back. It is not God who curses you, it is you cursing yourself; it is the law of God's universe in action.

THE ONE TRUE recognizable brand of a Christian is that they love others as they love themselves. This simplifies all of God's laws and everything he expects from us is fulfilled by this one commandment. Unfortunately, the church is not operating on this mandate from God, and there is confusion about who we really are. All the good works in the world mean nothing if we do not love others. Ultimately, this is our high calling: *"You will recognize them because they love each other."* Let's do it!

DAY 179   June 28

THROUGHOUT OUR LIVES, we all make mistakes. But the biggest mistake of all is to deny the mistake. When we defend our flesh over something it has done wrong, we reinforce the problem and give our flesh permission to continue in its folly. Always be willing to say, "I was wrong, I own it, and I am sorry." This wipes the slate clean. Remember that where there is no repentance, there is no forgiveness.

WE ARE CREATED to know what is good and what is not good. Are you willing to always say no to what is not good? No excuses? Every choice you make comes with a consequence! Good choices bring good consequences. Bad choices bring bad consequences. No excuses!

LIFE IS FULL of *somethings*. Learn to peacefully navigate through the different trials that are sure to present themselves throughout your life. Revel in the things that bring joy and problem-solve the trials. Whining and complaining only extends the problem and actually gives it more power. There is no utopia until we get to heaven.

THE JOY IS not just in the win or the finish line, but it is also in the journey. We will probably never be all that we should be, but run your race right to the end and strain to reach your highest calling. Joy comes in the overcoming of intense challenges, yet many won't even get in the race or they quit just before they reach the finish line. *"Run your race as if to win."*

WHEN THINGS IN your life have run amok and chaos swirls around you, learn to say, "God has this." If you can start your day with that thought and hang on to it throughout the day, you will have that peace that goes beyond understanding—the kind of peace the world cannot give, the kind that only God can give. And you'll be like a tree planted by the water that nothing can shake.

DEBASING YOURSELF WILL never bring you a blessing. In fact, it will bring a curse, and you will become exactly what you believe and say. Worse yet, your perceived unworthiness becomes an echo to the generations after you. Learn to love yourself and concentrate on your good qualities. *"In your weakness he is made strong."* Acknowledge God and let him work out the kinks.

July

MOST OF US trust God for the big things, but we think the little things don't matter to him, so we don't bother. Learn to trust God in absolutely everything. He's a big God and he can do everything at once. He is not too busy and he does care. Trust him for wisdom, direction, and the power to overcome. God is your constant companion—consult with him on every issue in your life. You'll be surprised at the results.

GOD HAS NOT abandoned this sin-wrecked world; you can see God in the flowers, in the sunshine, in the birds, in friendships, and in answered prayer. He is everywhere if you choose to see him. The earth and all its fullness belongs to God. Keep your eyes open for the hidden treasures that he scatters along the paths of those who call him Lord.

DAY 183   July 2

GOD WILL ALWAYS be victorious. It may appear at times that evil or bad is winning out, but in the end God's purposes will prevail! Be not deceived; nobody is getting by with anything, including you! As we sow, we will reap—whether good or bad. Be intentional about your choices and know that the whole of your life is a compilation of these choices. Nothing more and nothing less.

ALL OF US will lose someone or something that is dear to us, and grief is part of that program. God has equipped us to deal with grief, and while it is painful, it is a necessary process for restoration. However, we are not told to camp out in that valley of grief; we are told to walk through it and to forget the things that are behind and press into the things that are ahead. Holding on to grief will block the new life that God has planned for you.

DAY 184   July 3

LIFE IS SO precious! Don't waste it trying to live someone else's life, and don't let the opinions of others drown out who you are. Glean from others, but ultimately it is you and God that should rule the majority. Listen for the *"still, quiet voice"* that comes from within.

FEAR AND DOUBT are natural reactions. But when you put your trust in God and commit your ways to him, God will deliver you from all your fears and put a light on your path. God looks at the condition of your heart, and the heart will always trump your words. *"Create in me a clean heart."*

DAY 185   July 4

EVERYONE HAS PROBLEMS, so be nice! We all deal with something. And just because it appears someone has everything does not mean they don't hurt. We are told to *"count it all joy when we go through fiery trials."* Everyone has them. The difference is how we choose to handle them. God promises to walk with us through every single situation that may arise in our life. Walk it out as you trust God.

REMEMBER THAT NO advantage, small or large, is worth losing your integrity. Do not compromise even a little bit by letting any kind of dishonesty sneak into your life. Keeping your heart and life clean and upright will always produce a sweet harvest of abundance in every area of your life.

DAY 186   July 5

DO NOT BE afraid to recognize your own errors. Your shortcomings do not diminish your character but provide a place for courage, humility, growth, and personal depth. It is beneficial to be aware of your weaknesses as well as your strengths. Conduct your life using your strengths, but be honest about your shortcomings and ask God to help you in those areas. God can work your biggest deficit into your greatest asset if you allow it."

BELIEVE GOD FOR something that seems impossible! His Word says, *"Only believe."* If there is a situation in your life that seems impossible, give God a chance by standing on his Word. Then *do not* set a time limit! It will come to pass in due season. *"Only believe!"*

DAY 187   July 6

EVERY ONE OF us will have to confront fear at one time or another. Being afraid does not mean you are weak. Sometimes it just happens. The main thing is that even in light of fear we still choose to be courageous. True courage is taking action and doing what is right, even when we are afraid. God's Word says, *"Be strong and courageous."* It's not what you *feel* but what you *do* that makes a hero.

FAITH AND PATIENCE are what will bring you to fruition. If you have the confidence that God will do what he says he will, and you exercise patience, you will see the fulfillment of your dreams. But if you waiver or give up, you will not receive from God. Don't allow anything to move you off of what God's Word says about your situation. *"After you have done all you know to do, stand and believe."*

DAY 188 July 7

IF FAITH SHOWS up in what you do, you will prove your faith, and faith will bring about miracles. Just saying you have faith is not good enough; you have to put action to your faith. *"Faith without works is dead."* Faith is what makes everything work. Latch on to the hope of living by faith and activate it with positive works.

"THERE IS A friend who sticks closer than a brother." There are times that we have a friend who will stick by us even more than our family. God knits hearts together and many times actually replaces our biological family with more kindred spirits. We are called to love everyone, but we are not called to like everyone. Always respect and pray for your family, but you do not have to hang around with them. Many times loving them from a distance is the healthy choice.

DAY 189   July 8

YOU ARE GOING to be tested in life and when you pass the test, blessings will follow. We all have issues and need God, so don't let your flesh mess with your mind. God does hear your cry and he does care. Trials and troubles will always befall believers, but remember that God takes pleasure in the prosperity of his children, and prosperity is not always monetary; it is in every area of your life. Be encouraged.

NEGATIVE THOUGHTS ARE the weakest when they first appear, so destroy them before they have a chance to get a foothold in your life. If you allow yourself to dwell on negative thoughts, they will grow just like something you feed. Cast a negative thought out immediately. Do not give it any place in your life.

DAY 190   July 9

TO APPROACH LIFE like it is one big game that you always have to win is a delusional, hopeless fantasy. Only what's done for God will endure. In the end, a superficial life will leave you empty and unfulfilled. Your happiest life is the one God planned for you. Seek his direction as you go.

NEVER, EVER LET your critics determine what you do. No matter what you do, critics will always question you. Follow your heart. Even when we know what is right, critics can cause us to doubt. I can't even imagine how many people have been cheated out of their dreams because someone told them they couldn't do it Never, ever listen to critics!

Day 191   July 10

PEOPLE OFTEN TEND to give *coincidence* the credit for something God has done. Always remember this: If you have prayed and asked God specifically for something and it comes to pass, do not call this a coincidence. Good "coincidences" are always from God. When you pray, expect to receive and then remember to say thank you—not to the universe, or to chance, or good luck, but to God, who is *"the giver of all good gifts."* Those who expect miracles from God will receive them.

THE CONDITION AT your birth does not determine the outcome of your life. Many of us were born into a troubled family situation, but this does not mean it is your lot in life. The good news is that God says *"we are blessed according to the work of our hands and the words of our mouth."* This is a principle of life and it works for everyone, even those who do not serve God. The principles are for everyone, while the promises only belong to those who serve God. So keep your hands busy and watch what comes out of your mouth.

STUDIES HAVE SHOWN that there are fifty-one different illnesses that are caused by anger. Left unchecked, anger will make you sick. When you allow yourself to explode, there is a high risk of having a heart attack within two hours. Anger is caused by fear, frustration, or hurt. Recognize and admit your reason for anger and then communicate. *"A wise man holds his tongue while a fool mouths off."* A quick temper will always cost you something. Calculate the cost and remember that *"anger will never accomplish the purposes of God."*

CHARLES DICKENS SAID, "Reflect upon your present blessings—of which every man has many—not on your past misfortunes, of which all men have some." This statement is so true. Take the time today to think about your blessings and keep your mind focused on the sweet things that are in your life. Remember that what you focus on is what will be magnified. *"If there be anything noble or pure, think on these things."*

Day 193   July 12

"IF YOU SEEK God and his righteousness before you seek anything else, all other things will be added to you." Striving to have the things that you want will never bring true happiness; the more you get, the more you will want. But if you put all of your attention on God and his will for you, he will make sure that every need you have will be met, and all of the desires of your heart will come to pass.

INSTEAD OF LOOKING at the things that are wrong in your life, start praising God for the things that are right. There is always something to be grateful for, and remember whatever you focus on is what will grow. Focus on what is right, not what is wrong. God's Word says that *"whatever things are pure or noble or lovely, think on these things."*

DAY 194   July 13

WHEN GOD CONFRONTS and corrects us, it is always for restoration and improvement. He corrects those whom he loves. Sometimes we think that something that's going on in our life must be from the devil, when in fact it is actually our Father in heaven, much like a parent taking action when they see their beloved child doing something that will harm them. God is a good God and he always means well for us. If you really trust God he will fine-tune your character, and sometimes the fine-tuning is painful.

THERE ARE MANY times that we just flat-out cannot understand God. Talking to God about your issues is fine, but we need to tell God that we trust him even when we don't understand. Learn to simply live by God's promises, believe them, quote them, and stand on them. Get to a place in your life where you can say, "Okay, God, I can't figure this out, but I know that you have a plan and I trust that plan." *"Those who put their trust in God will never be disappointed."*

*"**THE PREPARATION OF** the heart belongs to man, but the answer of the tongue is from the Lord."* We can and should have dreams, but if something is not God's will for you, all the preparations in the world will not make it happen. If we try to build something without God in it, we are building on sand and it cannot withstand the storms of life. Make your plans, do your part, then trust God for the outcome.

WE ARE SUPPOSED to believe God for everything, but God's Word also says to *"do all you know to do,"* and then stand and believe. Sometimes I think we stand and believe and expect God to do it all when we don't do what we know to do first. Be sure that you are doing your part in every situation, trusting God for direction as you go by putting action to your faith.

DAY 196 July 15

GRATITUDE UNLOCKS THE fullness of life! When you are grateful for even the small things, life is delightful. Every twist and turn brings a treasured memory as you choose to focus on the sweet, lovely, noble, fun, beautiful things in life. Gratitude is the best gift of all!

BE WILLING TO receive correction. We all have areas of weakness, and if you deny your weakness, you cannot change or grow, and God cannot fix something that you refuse to acknowledge. This is not the same as getting into condemnation. It is simply the wisdom in a man to recognize his own flaws and his desire to be a better person. *"There is no condemnation to those who are in Christ Jesus."*

WHEN YOUR MISSION in this life is centered on you, you will always have trouble. Get your mind off yourself and put it on others who need your prayers and your help. Pulling inward will always intensify what you are feeling. God's Word says, *"Pray one for the other that you might be healed."* Need healing? Find someone with a problem similar to yours and pray for them.

DO ALL YOU can, when you can, and live your life right to the end. The word *retirement* is not in the Bible. Age is only a number, and we should continue to operate just like we always have until the day we go home to be with the Lord. The moment people begin to profess they are old, life changes. How old would you be if you didn't know how old you are? Live your life accordingly!

CHRISTIANITY IS NOT a religion; it's a life-transforming relationship with Jesus. Christianity is personal, and although church is a part of the Christian life, it is not the main part. Many people attend church and really never get to know their Savior, while Christianity is a personal relationship with God. Religion often involves pride, exclusion, and judgmental man-made rules. God loves the church and reminds us to *"not forsake the gathering of ourselves together."* But be aware of Pharisees who attend church for the wrong reasons.

HOPE IS SO important for the well-being of every human. Hope thinks, *It will be better in a minute.* Help keep hope alive for others by reminding them that things will get better. We all need to hear words of encouragement. On average, eight people will hear something negative, while only three will hear something positive. Shame on us! Be one who brings a good report. Always keep hope alive.

DAY 199   July 18

DON'T LIVE A little bitty boring life just because you don't want to take a chance, or because you are stuck in a rut that, though boring, is safe. Choose to live boldly and incredibly! Following the path of least resistance will never accomplish greatness or a remembered legacy. God has called his people to *"be strong and courageous,"* to blaze a trail that others want to follow—a trail scattered with outrageous good deeds, creative thinking, souls won to the Lord, and yes, lots of laughter and fun as you serve God.

WHEN YOU STOP chasing the wrong things, you give the right things a chance to catch you. *Selah!* Examine your life for those things that require much of your time but have gotten you nowhere. Sometimes you just need to walk life out and not struggle so much. God promises to direct the paths of his people. Try to let go and let God. I know that sounds glib, but if you do it, it will really work!

GOD'S WORD SAYS, *"It is not good for man to be alone."* Accept the friendship that each individual offers you. We are all uniquely different, and it is rare that one person can fulfill all of your needs. Enjoy the strengths that each offer and do not compare one to the other. Remember that *"those who have friends must show themselves friendly."* Your friends are nothing more than a reflection of the kind of friend you are.

GOD REQUIRES US to *"do justice, love mercy and walk humbly before him."* Basically, these three requirements encompass all of what God expects of us. To do justice means to always be fair and do what is right. To love mercy is to always forgive others as well as yourself. To walk humbly before him means to always acknowledge his omnipotence and realize that without him we are nothing. And that, my friends, is the simplicity of serving God.

*"**THE INTEGRITY OF** the upright will guide them, but the perversity of the unfaithful will destroy them."* Walking in integrity will actually define a clear path before you; it will shine a light on your path. You just can't miss when you choose to always do what you know to be right. Perverse choices will never be successful choices. It may seem you are getting by with things for a time, but it will come back to bite you.

FAITH AND RIGHTEOUS living is passed down from generation to generation. Our lifestyles will affect our children. Whether it is good or bad, it is impactful to all the young people in our life. Little acts of kindness can change a life. Light up the lives of those around you by always doing what is right. Actions speak louder than words. *"By their fruit you will know them."*

LIFE CAN BE going along beautifully and all of a sudden something can happen to change things. Reality is real, and running away from it, getting angry, or trying to sweep things under the rug does not change reality. Changes and losses are just a part of life. Embrace your new reality and don't spend your days comparing to what you have lost. *"Sorrow may last for a night, but joy will come in the morning."* Expect it and accept it!

WE ARE ONLY as strong as the people we surround ourselves with. *"Be not deceived, bad company corrupts good behavior."* Take an intentional look at your close friends and you will see in them what others see in you. Does that rest easy on your mind? If not, make some changes.

DAY 203   July 22

YOU CANNOT MAKE yourself feel something you don't feel, but you can make yourself do right in spite of your feelings. No matter how much we try to rationalize why we made a bad choice, it will not make it right. Always go with your God-given instinct. There is such a sense of well-being in a life of integrity.

TEARS AND LAUGHTER have the same impact in releasing pain. Of course, it is always more fun to laugh away our sorrows, but when the pain is so great that even laughter won't come, allow yourself to cry. The more we push pain down, the more it hurts. Face your pain and allow God to heal you with cleansing tears.

"THE DILIGENT HAND shall rule," and *"if you're faithful with a little, you will rule over much."* These two proverbs encompass the keys to success. Faithful and diligent. In other words, stay put and work hard! This works in every area of your life—marriage, friendship, business, school, everywhere.

THERE ARE HUNDREDS of fears known to man, yet there are only two fears that we are born with: fear of falling, and fear of loud noises. All other fears are learned behavior. Fear is our worst enemy because it is the opposite of faith, and faith is what activates God's promises. God's Word says, *"Call unto me and I will deliver you out of all your fears."* It works!

A BITTER HEART is much worse than a physical injury. The key to a successful life is not what happens to you, but how you *handle* what happens to you. We have all seen people who have had incredible physical injuries, yet they continue to joyfully participate in life. Then there are those who become bitter, and even though their body is whole, they wither away. *"Happy is he who puts his hope in the Lord."* No matter what your lot in life, *"rejoice, again I say rejoice."*

IF YOU DO what you do well, with a good attitude, and you choose to become excellent at what you do, you will stand out in the crowd. People listen to others based on their performance. When you perform in excellence, you will have a platform that no one else will have and you will never "fail" in life. Everyone will want to hear what you have to say and will want to do business with you. It's your choice!

Day 206   July 25

"THE RIGHTEOUS CRY out and God delivers them out of all their troubles." What an amazing promise! God tells us to remind him of what he said. Do it God's way and remind him as you cry out to him for his deliverance. We all have troubles in this life, and God gives us the antidote—it's pretty simple. Your part is to cry out; the rest is up to him. I love it!

KNOWLEDGE AND WISDOM are not the same thing. Knowledge is taught by man, and wisdom is taught by God. *"The fear of the Lord is the beginning of wisdom."* Knowledge is running rampant in our world, but *"one day every knee shall bow."*

DAY 207 July 26

YOU CANNOT BE pitiful and powerful at the same time. Choose to be powerful. Just because you have a setback does not mean you have lost. Setbacks are not failures; they are educators for your future. Refuse to be defeated. Keep moving forward, drawing on the things that caused you to fail before. Don't focus on them as deficits, but think of them as assets that will help you avoid the same mistake again. The most important thing you have going for you is refusing to give up.

OUR BLESSINGS IN life are usually not "out there" somewhere. More times than not they are right under our nose. Many times we are so busy scanning the horizon for that faraway blessing that we miss what is right at our feet. Pay attention to your lot in life; it is where you are and who you are with, and many times it means we have to make lemonade out of lemons. But God will always give increase to those who are faithful with what they have.

Day 208 July 27

ALWAYS DO WHAT is right and you will never have to feel guilty. Guilt comes when you are not honoring your core values. No matter what happens in your life, if you make good, godly choices and treat people with respect, guilt has no place in your life. Guilt is a tormentor and will cause you to do things you should not do and to make choices that you should not make. Make restitution when possible, ask God for forgiveness, and shake it off.

THE IMAGE THAT you see will define your life. What do you see? Make a decision to look at the image of victory. Keep your eyes and your mind on things that are lovely, beautiful, noble, and praiseworthy. The world is definitely full of carnage and debauchery but it has at least an equal amount of beauty, and this beauty becomes part of the eye of the beholder. Keep the image of that beauty in your mind and do not allow it to be diluted by letting your mind or your eye stray. *"The good man brings out of his treasure what is good, while the evil man brings out what is evil."*

DAY 209   July 28

WHEN YOU HEAR the Word of God and put it into practice, you are building your life on a rock. When troubles come—and they always will—you will be like a tree planted by the water that nothing will shake. If your life is built on the ways of the world, it is built on sand and will crumble under the pressures of life. Don't be fooled by the glamour of the world; it is temporal and full of disappointment. *"Those who put their hope in God will never be disappointed."*

LEARN TO BE comfortable in your circumstances. We all have issues that we must deal with, and it doesn't do any good to focus on them or lament over them. There will always be things in your life that are daunting. If you have asked God to remove them, don't doubt that he will. Decide to be content in whatever place you find yourself. Keep moving forward with an optimistic expectation as you walk out your journey.

Day 210   July 29

THERE ARE NONE more blind than those who refuse to see. I think all of us participate at some time or another in this stubbornness that stunts our life, refusing to even consider that we might be wrong or that there might be a better way. We cling to our puny ideas and think we know it all. Life should be changing and moving, and we should be learning new things every day.

OUTWARD SIGNS OF a hard life do not mean things aren't good. What matters more is how we handle the hard life. Never compare yourself one to the other. God has a plan for each of us that is unique and detailed. Make a decision to work through the issues of life with a joyful and upbeat character. Life is full of peaks and valleys, but God promises to walk through the valleys with us. *"Be strong and courageous."*

YOUR SUCCESSES EARN you the right to have people listen to you. No matter where you are in life, if you will strive to be excellent you will float to the top like rich cream on milk. It does not matter what job you have, you will be promoted! People in authority are always drawn to people who operate in an excellent manner. I believe that when God tells us in his Word to *"rise and shine,"* he is telling us to conduct our lives with an excellence that will glorify him. Begin with excellence and then go for it!

YOUR FEARS WILL tell you where you do not trust God. Almost half of our fears are about the future, over which we have no control. Some are about the past, to which we can never go back. What a waste of time! God tells us to concern ourselves about today, and tomorrow will take care of itself. Embrace God's way by using God's Word. *"Fear cannot be where there is faith."*

Day 212   July 31

DON'T LOSE YOUR cool over some insignificant, temporary something. If you can't keep your peace in a small thing, you will never be able to stand and believe for the big blessings God has planned for you. Many times it's nothing more than a choice that prevents us from going to a place of oppression, disappointment, or frustration. Plan ahead how you will handle trivial life happenings.

YEP, IT'S PERFECTLY okay and even suggested that you enjoy your life and still have fun even when you have a problem, while life is raging around you. Never feel guilty because you are able to laugh even in the midst of tragedy. Actually, this is the best thing you can do. Sometimes we just need to laugh at the absurdities of life. God's Word says, *"A merry heart does good like a medicine."* Find a friend that you can laugh with and then just let go. You will feel so good afterward.

August

QUIET YOUR SPIRIT and do not allow confusion to get a foothold in your life. Remember that confusion is never from God. Make decisions based on what you know to be right and then relax. God takes over from there. *"Be still and know that I am God."*

A NEGATIVE ATTITUDE makes a person mean-spirited, and we cannot have God's best when we are negative. Draw a line in the sand and refuse to allow yourself to be negative. We have the power to choose our own attitude, and remember that your altitude depends on your attitude. Think yourself happy.

DAY 214   August 2

REFUSE TO DO life alone. A lack of satisfying relationships has been proven to take people out sooner than overeating or smoking., Close relationships will impact your world and the world around you. Invest in your relationships because you will only get out of them what you are willing to put in. *"Woe to him who is alone, because when he falls there is no one to pick him up."*

WE SELDOM UNDERSTAND our trials at the time. We may even feel like failures and wonder why God allows suffering. But as time passes we learn to look back and see how he worked things for good and how every trial enhanced our life and drove us closer to God. If we trust God through every test, our relationship with him will grow and our perseverance will become more steady.

DAY 215   August 3

WE ARE BULLETPROOF until things get rough and then we call out to God. We could eliminate a lot of mishaps in our life if we learned to *"acknowledge God in all our ways and let him make our path straight."*

JUST AS THE fruit on the tree is smaller if we do not prune it, such is our life when we get too busy. When we get too much going, the fruit of our life is small and sour. Be selective with your time and you will be able to produce sweet, juicy fruit every day of your life. If you honor God first, all other things will be added unto you—including time.

DAY 216   August 4

DON'T SAVE THINGS for special occasions, because every day is a special occasion. Enjoy and savor every day, every hour, every moment. "Live like it is your last day, love like you've never been hurt, and dance like no one is watching." And remember to thank God for everything!

WHEN YOU LOOK for spiritual growth in your life, don't stand impatiently in front of a mirror. Take the long view. Defending your character flaws only reinforces them. It is so easy to defend those things in us that create problems, even when we know they are wrong. To be unwilling to take note of those things that rob us of the joy that life can bring is not only fruitless, it is downright insane. We all have flaws, but *"God is faithful to finish the work that he has started in us."*

THERE ARE TIMES when things are over so overwhelming that we don't even know what to pray. Remember that God knows our needs even before we ask, and although Jesus tells us that *"we have not because we ask not,"* it is not necessary to carry on with a long, eloquent prayer. I love the simplicity of my "help me" prayer or "help them" prayer. When your prayer list is long, sometimes you just need to call out the person's name; God knows the rest.

EVERYONE HAS THINGS out of order, including you and me, yet we are so quick to identify something ugly in someone's life. Do not judge by a few small things in the life of an individual; rather, look at the whole of their life. Take the plank out of your own eye before trying to remove the speck from your brother's eye. As you judge others, you yourself will be judged. Be kind!

DAY 218   August 6

THERE IS A time for everything under the sun, *"a time to weep and a time to laugh; a time to mourn and a time to dance."* Allow yourself to go through the trials of life, knowing that there is an end to them. Remember that when you have experienced deep sorrow and mourning, you become more capable of receiving and living great joy.

DESPERATE TIMES CALL for desperate measures. Establish yourself on the solid ground of faith, as you cannot rely on your own efforts in the natural realm to receive maximum benefits in this life. The world's security is flimsy at best and is built on sand. It has no solid ground to withstand the pressures of life. Build your life on the rock of faith and it will withstand anything that comes your way.

FEAR AND DREAD will cause you to live in shallowness. A decision based on fear will never be the right decision. Dig deep within yourself to find the strength and courage that God promises his people and that must be utilized by faith in order to gain victory over your circumstances. *"Fear not!"*

SURROUND YOURSELF WITH things that make you happy. You have the ability to change your environment. It doesn't take money or stuff, it just takes an attitude of gratitude and a little elbow grease and creative thinking as you fluff up your surroundings. If you make the most of what you already have, I promise you God will give you increase. Sitting around whining and wallowing in self-pity will only dig the pit deeper. *"If you're faithful with a little, you will get a lot."*

PEOPLE'S TENDENCY IS to hide and defend their errors, seeking refuge in darkness where they indulge in denial, self-pity, or self-righteousness, often blaming others for their problems. Be willing to step up to the plate and admit your errors. Darkness can't be where there's light, and light always brings healing and restoration.

"OUT OF THE abundance of the heart, the mouth speaks." The heart gives the real meaning to your words, and your words will reveal your true heart. Listen to yourself as well as to others. Words are a powerful tool and can actually change a life. Be intentional with your words, remembering that *"pleasant words are like a honeycomb, sweet to the soul and healing to all the flesh."*

DAY 221   August 9

THINKING SOMETHING BAD is bad enough, but once it comes out of your mouth, you give it power. Before shooting your mouth off, use a filter of wisdom. Think before you speak and don't say everything you think; many things are better left unsaid. "Better to remain silent and be thought a fool than to speak and remove all doubt."

EVEN THOUGH OUR pathways twist and turn through stony landscapes, if we look back, we will see thousands of miles of miracles and answered prayers. Life is full of potholes and bumps in the road. Travel your journey with a confidence that our God goes with you and will see you through every mishap. Watch for the little signs of his presence in your life. It is usually in the little things wherein lie his miracles.

DAY 222   August 10

WE GET THE most out of life when we learn to connect the dots. This allows us to see the whole picture. Most hurts and disappointments are caused by a choice we made. Even when we are a victim of the choices of others, we still have choices to make that profoundly affect our life. Ask God to help you daily.

PEOPLE ASK, "HOW do you know when you hear God?" We hear God urging us in our spirits, or by reading his Word. We also hear him through the mouths of others. Sometimes people are not even aware that God is using them to speak to you, and other times they may tell you that they have a word for you from God. Before proceeding with a perceived word from God, be sure these three proofs are in place: (1) It must be scriptural; it cannot be something that is outside of God's Word. (2) Circumstances must be right before following through. *"There is a time and season for everything under the sun."* (3) You must have a witness in your own spirit. *"A truth is established in the mouth of two or three witnesses."* Even if you get two out of three of these, do not proceed. Wait until all three of these things are in place. Then listen up and go for it!

DAY 223   August 11

IF YOU FIND yourself surrounded with friends that annoy you, you probably need to take a closer look at yourself. Remember that to have friends you must show yourself friendly. Friendship is a sweet responsibility. It is also a commitment to be available for your friend even when it's not convenient for you. "A friend in need is a friend indeed."

OUR OWN INIQUITIES entrap us. Throughout our journey through life, we will all do things that are not right. I call this the "fallen man syndrome." But the key is to make an immediate correction before it has a chance to ensnare us. Similar to quicksand, if you only go up to your ankles and don't stay in it too long, it is easy to get out, but if you let yourself sink in up to your waist, you are snared like a rabbit in a trap. Clean your slate daily and start anew each morning.

DAY 224   August 12

WHATEVER IS IN a man's heart will eventually come out of his mouth. Pay attention to your own words and the words of others. The mouth has trouble keeping secrets. The mind thinks it, the heart feels it, the mouth says it, and the rest of the body will follow. Be careful with words—they carry the power of life and death, and you will eat the fruit of your lips. Check your heart often and ask God to help you set it in order. Your thought process is what establishes your heart. Cast down all wild imaginings, speak only positive, edifying words, and watch your life change for the better!

PSALM 138 SAYS, *"I will save you in the midst of your troubles."* It doesn't matter what your trouble is, God is a big God and can change things in an instant. He says it will be done unto you as you believe. If you are having trouble believing God, ask him to help you with your unbelief. Remember that you will eat the fruit of your words, so speak positive words that confirm what you are believing.

DAY 225   August 13

IT IS IMPORTANT to maintain peace in your personal environment even when chaos abounds. Protect yourself by establishing internal order and by avoiding chaotic encounters as much as possible. Do what you can to stay calm even in the midst of a storm. Trust God at all times and remember that we are called to a life of peace.

GOD GIVES ALL of us a plot in life that we must go in and possess. Every single plot has giants that must be fought in order to take possession. Many people choose not to fight the giants. They feel over-whelmed, lazy, or they walk in fear and never get what God has ordained for them. Be willing to fight for the things that matter. Procrastination, slothfulness, and fear are thieves of life. *"Fear not, go in and possess the land that is rightfully yours!"*

DAY 226   August 14

THERE ARE THOUSANDS of promises in the Bible given to those who serve God. However, there are principles that are activated in even the lives of the wicked if the caveat attached to the principle is adhered to. For instance: *"You are blessed according to the work of your hands."* It does not matter who you are, if you work hard, your hands will be blessed. But promises such as *"all of your children will be taught of the Lord"* are the heritage of those who serve God. Study the Word to make yourselves approved and then remind God of these wonderful promises that belong to you. *"You have not because you ask not."*

HUMILITY IS NOT thinking poorly of yourself but simply realizing that you need God. Humility is not a place of weakness, but strength. The foolish man thinks he can do everything without God, and this man will surely fall, while the man of humble character realizes that God is his strength, and he will never fall. *"God opposes the proud but gives grace to the humble."*

DAY 227   August 15

BICKERING AND DISPUTES are not always bad. In fact, many times they can actually strengthen a relationship. They can establish what is needed to correct an issue. It is healthy to discuss something that is bothering you rather than acting like nothing is wrong and sweeping it under the rug. Keeping it in will create resentment and eventually the problem will surface in subliminal ways. Just remember to be fair and listen to the other side, and never hit below the belt! *"The prudent word of a wise man will get him out of difficulties."*

RATHER THAN LOOKING at the problem, look at the promises. There is a promise provided in the Bible for absolutely everything that could possibly happen to you, but you must find the promise and apply it. If you have never studied the Bible and you do not know where to find these valuable antidotes, just Google it! We Google everything else. God tells us to *"bring him in remembrance of his word."* So follow his instructions. Find the promise and apply it to your situation. This puts your problem in God's hands. You cannot do things your way and expect God to follow your instructions.

DAY 228   August 16

WE CANNOT RECEIVE if we are unwilling to give. *"As you give, it is given unto you."* This is a principle of God and it works for the just and the unjust equally. If you are needy, give to someone else who needs something. When God says that it is *"more blessed to give than to receive"* it can sound so strange. I remember when I used to think that was impossible. But today I totally understand the meaning of that scripture. It is truly more blessed to give than to receive. Try it!

YOU OWE IT to yourself and your loved ones to do your best, not in comparison to others but only in comparison to your own set of abilities. It is discouraging and a waste of time to compete with others. Your responsibility lies in maxing out the gifts that were given to you. We are all special and unique in our own way, and I believe one of the biggest deterrents to success is wanting to be like others instead of savoring who we are. It is great to try to pattern yourself after a mentor with similar giftings, but ultimately you need to be yourself. This is where your true success lies. Believe that you are *"fearfully and wonderfully made."*

WHEN YOU ARE stressed out, your whole body will react with loss of memory, trouble concentrating, nausea, chest pains, overeating, moodiness, diarrhea, shortness of breath, negative thoughts, poor judgment, aches and pains of all sorts, and on and on. The Word says that we can overcome stress by keeping our troubled heart focused on God and his promises rather than on our problems. Your whole body will react to your focus, and remember that *"God loves to display his power in the lives of those who completely trust him."* I love, love, love that promise!

"AS MUCH AS possible, be at peace with all men." Keep your feet on the path of peace throughout your life. There are some unavoidable people in your life who will rattle your cage. Sometimes this is simply iron sharpening iron, but other times you need to separate yourself from these people as much as possible and do your part to maintain the life of peace that we are called to live."

YOUR ACTIONS WILL always follow your beliefs. Our belief system actually controls our life, and if you expose yourself to trash, you will eventually believe it and react accordingly. Surround yourself with wise, edifying people, and be careful what you see and read. *"Bad company corrupts good character."*

HURRIEDNESS CAN BE the death of kindness. Sometimes our life can get so big and so complex that we rush around like chickens with our heads cut off and miss all the little treasures that are strewn along our path. We miss the little acts of kindness that we could give to others because we are so busy that we don't notice. While heaven is our final destination goal, the journey of this life is our earthly reward.

OPPORTUNITY DOESN'T ALWAYS come at an opportune time, it usually comes when you least expect it. If you're not prepared to be spontaneous at these times, you will miss the window of opportunity. The old adage "Think long, think wrong" is usually accurate. Overthinking will often present so many problems that you won't take the chance. If you have a confirmation in your spirit, step out in faith; the worst that can happen is it will fail. No guts, no glory!

BE GENEROUS IN your conclusions of others. When you judge, you don't know the whole story. There is a lot more to the actions of others than what you see or presume. *"Love is gentle, kind, patient, it endures all, is not jealous or haughty. And it does not puff itself up."* If you call yourself a Christian, act accordingly.

WE ARE NOT called to like everyone. In fact, there are some people that just don't blend well together. This does not make them bad people, it just means that we have to love them from a distance and treat them with respect and kindness. I think the truest love of all is when you really, really *like* someone, and you love them as well.

"A FOOL IS deceived by his own foolishness." The condition of man is such that we see what we want to see. It does not come naturally to randomly see what we don't believe in; it is something we have to do intentionally. Make choices to at least listen to all opposing issues and then logically make your decision about what you believe. Never let a stubborn, made-up mind block you from being teachable.

DAY 233   August 21

THE HUMAN VOICE can bring comfort, especially if it is from someone you trust. Use your voice to comfort, console, and encourage your loved ones. The Bible says that God's people hear his voice. There is nothing more comforting than the voice of God, and we can hear it by reading his Word and praying. Listen for that still, quiet voice that says, *Stop, go this way*. Just as you need to block out the sounds around you to hear the voice of a person, it is also important to be silent and listen to God. *"Be still and know that I am God."*

GOD SAYS TO *"be quick to listen and slow to speak."* A quick temper will magnify foolishness. Take the time to process things before shooting your mouth off. The old adage of counting to ten before speaking is still a good idea. When you are angry, "less is more," so the less you say, the better off you will be. Much of communication is nonverbal, so watch your antics as well. All of us will experience anger in our lives, but it is our choice how we handle it. Where there is no contender, there is no contention.

DAY 234   August 22

GOD'S WORD SAYS, *"Be ye therefore perfect, even as your father in heaven is perfect."* How are we supposed to be perfect when we all fall so short? I have come to a conclusion on this matter, and it is this: just as the small green nub on a fruit tree is not yet a beautiful piece of fruit, it is still perfect as it transitions into the final product. So are we as God continues to finish the work he has started in us. If we are trusting God and growing, even a little bit, we are in a perfect state of transition. You are therefore perfect.

MOST PEOPLE EXPECT little from God, ask little, and therefore receive little and are content with little. We serve a big God. He can do everything at once. *"You have not because you ask not."* Ask God and then expect that he will answer. What we expect is what we usually get.

Day 235   August 23

IF YOU HAVE issues that you are struggling with, don't keep them a secret. When we keep things in the dark they tend to appear scarier and bigger and the load or guilt is heavier. Share your burden with a trusted friend, a pastor, or a counselor. Don't let shame or embarrassment prevent you from getting help. The Word says, *"Confess your sins one to the other that you may be healed."*

IT IS NOT the devil or the world that blocks our blessing, it is usually us. We have a book of instructions that gives us the answer to everything, and yet many times we choose to do exactly the opposite of what God says will make life work. If we follow the Bible and study to make ourselves approved, life will flow at its peak. Read and study the Bible.

DAY 236   August 24

CIRCUMSTANCES AND PEOPLE don't make us who we are, they reveal who we are. No one and no thing can make us angry, greedy, envious, hateful, or turn us into lawless people. "The devil made me do it" is not a true statement. People like to blame things on the devil when they have caused their own problems. Own up to the part you play in every negative situation in your life. Blaming others will never get things worked out; it is a dead-end street that causes division with loved ones. *"A house divided will fall."*

THERE IS A time to live and a time to die, and every one of us will have to deal with the passing of someone we love in our lifetime. Those who know God pass on to something much better than they're leaving, but that doesn't ease the grief of those left behind. Comfort yourself with the thought that you will see them again one day.

BREAK LOOSE AND free yourself from dysfunctional people who are experts at meeting their own needs at the expense of yours. Do not let people stay in your life who trample on your feelings or behave badly. Set clear boundaries so that you do not get caught up in their maze of madness or feel responsible for their life choices or consequences. It is wonderful to help others when you can but ultimately we are all responsible for our own lives.

IN THE BIG picture of things, financial wealth is not the key to happiness. In fact, its importance falls way below some of the more solid things in life. The Word says that *"the blessing of God makes rich without any sorrow."* Many times riches bring sorrow, worry, and sleepless nights. Not everyone is going to have huge financial blessings, but I do know this: if we do our part and *"seek God first, all other things will be added unto us."*

GOD DOES NOT send trouble into our life, but he does use our messes to work toward good and to bring us into another space. God promises that he will never violate our right to choose. Those choices often take us to places that are not planned for our life, but through all the wrong choices, if we put our faith in God, we will always land on our feet.

"I WILL INSTRUCT you and teach you in the way you should go." When God directs us, it is not just for the benefit of the short term, he is looking at the whole picture, and his guidance will lead us in a direction that may not look like it's right for the moment but ultimately is leading us to a place he wants us to be. If you have asked for guidance, trust that you are where you are supposed to be.

WHEN YOU STAND praying, if you hold aught against anyone, forgive so that your prayers may be heard in heaven. Do you realize the ramifications of unforgiveness? The Scriptures are true, and they say that if you hold unforgiveness, your prayers will not be heard. Have you been praying for something that has not come to pass—something that God promises and yet has eluded you? Check your heart. Remember that God does not give any exceptions to this rule; he knows your hurt and your heart. Make your proclamation of forgiveness and he will do the rest.

DON'T LET YOUR history define your destiny. We all have things in our past that we are ashamed of, but this does not mean we have to carry guilt forward. Most of the time those very things that shamed us are the very things that God uses as a testimony to help others. Our testimony is one of the key components to overcoming the wiles of the world.

DAY 240   August 28

LOVE OTHERS AS you love yourself. If you have a loathing for yourself, you can never love others properly. You will only be able to love others with the depth that you are able to love yourself. This does not mean that you should be arrogant and pompous. It simply means that you accept the unique character that God created you with—even with all of your quirks. Pamper yourself and treat yourself with love. You are unique and special!

"A FRIEND STICKS closer than a brother." People will come and go throughout our life, and most of them are only there for a season. We need to learn from them, enjoy our season with them, and lovingly release them. You will easily recognize your lifetime friends, because they stick by you no matter what happens in your life. They are the ones who are there to pick you up when you fall, to cry with you when you cry, and to laugh with you through the joys of life. They are the ones who sharpen you, even through trials and disagreements. It is said that you can count these treasured friends on one hand. Love them well and give thanks for these special people who have chosen to walk with you through this journey called "life."

DAY 241   August 29

HURRY CAN DESTROY your joy. Don't just skim life. Unclutter and savor your life! There is always something to do, and worthy projects abound. However, you can't do everything, and it is foolish to try. You will never do your best when you're rushing around trying to fit everything in. Prioritize your life. Slow down and pay attention to the things that really matter.

IF THE BIBLE does not make sense to you, it is because it can be compared to a box of intricate puzzle pieces that must be tediously put in their proper place to form the intended picture. Each piece fits perfectly with the corresponding mate, and if the sections are looked at independently, they often do not make sense. Thus, a person looks at one scripture and is baffled. It takes a lifetime to assemble this incredibly beautiful picture that surpasses anything on earth. *"Study to show thyself approved."*

THE WORD SAYS, *"Woe to him who does evil to someone who has never done anything but good to them."* We do not have to worry about trying to get even with someone who has wronged us when we have done what is good to them. God says that justice will be done. Let God fight your battles. If you get in the ring and contend, God will let you, but there is a good chance you will lose. If you are on the side of "right," God will always fight for you, and you will always come out the victor.

YOUR BODY AND your life will align with the picture that you have of yourself in your own mind. Your life is always going to go toward the dominant picture of what you see. While it is good to critique and manage your character flaws, it is not good to throw yourself under the bus and lament over all of the tweaks in your character. Be kind to your own human frailties and allow God to finish the work that he has started in you.

DAY 243   August 31

THERE IS NO greater joy, nor greater reward, than to make a fundamental difference in someone's life. And besides that, it is so emotionally healthy to get outside of yourself. Use your gifts to bless others. *"We are blessed to be a blessing."*

*"**GUARD YOUR HEART** with all diligence, for out of it flows the issues of life."* We are responsible for guarding our own heart, God will not do it for us. Remember that what is in your heart will eventually surface. Be aware of what is in there because it will affect your life. It is not your circumstances that create your life; your real life lives inside of you. Check it at least as often as you do your face, your hair, your clothes, and all of the other outward things that we consider important, because in the end, it is only the heart that God sees.

September

WHEN WE KNOW what is right and we choose not to do it, it becomes a sin of "omission," which is equally as bad as the sin of commission—knowing something is wrong and doing it anyway. Just because we choose to do nothing, does not mean we are off the hook. If we know what to do and we don't do it, we are in sin. Every time we choose to do what is right, we are partnering with God and there is no better partner you can have. Sin separates us from God, and separation from God is the worst place you can find yourself. Always choose to do what you know is right.

PSALM 139 SAYS that *"God places his hand of blessing on your head."* I don't know about you, but that thought comforts and delights me. God's hand of blessing—wow! Get that visual picture of God's hand and walk in it. How can we go wrong!

DAY 245 September 2

KINDNESS IS THE true revealer of a person's greatness. Popularity is not a sign of greatness; in fact, many times popularity will cause people to become arrogant and prideful. The true sign of a champion and hero is a kind, caring, and meek spirit. In the end, *"the meek shall inherit the earth."* Ask God for a gentle, quiet, meek spirit. *"He always gives to those who ask."*

BE SENSITIVE TO your loved ones; treat them with the respect that you would give to a visitor in your home. Crass and crude actions are a turn-off. We all have an ugly side; never show it to others and especially not to your loved ones. Love is powerful but it is also very fragile. You will only be loved as you love. Give your best as you *"consider others more important than yourself."*

DAY 246   September 3

WHEN WE DON'T deal with situations as they arise, they pile one on top of the other and eventually overwhelm us and cause us to feel anxious and moody. If you have a situation in your life that you are dreading, do it first! "Eat the ugly frog first"—get the dreaded stuff out of the way. Procrastination is a thief of life, but a well-tended garden is the source of your abundant harvest.

TRANSPARENCY IS A beautiful attribute, and while you don't want to let all your ugly stuff hang out, you do want to share the real you with others without façade or pretension. Many times just sharing with a trusted friend works like a medicine. Secrets can make you sick. *"Confess your sins one to the other that you might be healed."*

Day 247   September 4

JUST BECAUSE SOMETHING is written does not make it true. We live in a culture that takes the written word in the newspapers, even in the gossip magazines, and believes it. A written word is nothing more than an opinion written by a man. The only written word that has proven itself to be absolute throughout the history of mankind is the Holy Bible. The test of time and the scrutiny of men have failed to ever prove error in this Word that is still the best-selling book in the world. *"It is a light upon your path."* Believe it!

PRAYER SHOULD BE a lifestyle, not our last hope. Prayer does not have to be eloquent. Share like you would with a friend. God says, *"You have not because you ask not."* Be specific and intentional in your prayers and watch God move in your favor. And be prepared, because it may be totally different than what you were expecting.

Day 248   September 5

OUR PROBLEM IN itself is not the problem—it's how we respond to our problem. It is our attitude and how we choose to view life that is our real problem. Choose to live life with gusto! Choose to love what is yours. Choose to accept your lot in life and not dwell on what you don't have. Choose to savor every moment of your life, whether you are climbing uphill or coasting down. Choose life!

IT IS SAID that God works in mysterious ways, and if you truly are submitted to him, and things happen that are hard to understand, it is usually God protecting you from something or moving you in a direction to position you for what he has for you. Do not beat down a closed door, or chase after someone who walked out of your life. *"God has a plan for your life—a plan to prosper you and not to harm you, a plan to give you hope and a future."* Even if you love something or someone, set it free; if it is yours, it will come back! Trust the process.

RIGHT THINKING BRINGS about right doing. We often cannot prevent things from coming into our mind, but we can stop them from getting a foothold. The Word says to *"cast down wild imaginings."* It is really simple not to allow things to get into your heart if you don't entertain the thought in your mind. When things come into the mind, they can be easily thrown out, but once they get down into the heart, they will cause us to act on them. *"As a man thinks, so he is."* Choose to be intentional with your thoughts.

THE THING THAT we attach ourselves to will determine who we become. God says that when we stay attached to him by obeying his commands, we will have joy, peace, patience, kindness, gratefulness, faithfulness, gentleness, self-control, and love. Wow! Isn't that what everyone is looking for in life? The truth is that if man would look to God for these treasures instead of drugs, alcohol, sex, and money, we would live in the beautiful world that God intended in the first place. *"God created man upright but he has devised many schemes."* Let's get back to basics!

Day 250   September 7

"HE HAS SHOWN you, O man, what is good; and what does the Lord require of you but to do justly, to love mercy, and to walk humbly with your God?" This is the simplicity of what God requires of us. It would behoove us to study and reflect on exactly what God means by this, because this scripture is the key to our blessings in life. We are to love God and be humble toward him and always do what is right where others are concerned.

A LACK OF confidence is really a lack of faith. Confidence is nothing more than believing that God can do what he says he can do. Confidence is faith activated. When we really believe who God is and what God can do, we will project an air of confidence that assures the world that everything in our life will work toward good no matter what the world throws at us. That is true confidence!

DAY 251   September 8

SOMETIMES WE GLAMORIZE and romanticize the past and we get pulled back instead of moving forward. Life should always be continuous movement, and there will be valleys as well as crests. Everything in life will eventually pass away and be replaced with something new. Today should never have to compete with the memories of yesterday. Choose to savor the moment and simply smile at the sweet memories you have of yesterday.

YOU CANNOT BRING a burden too heavy for God to lift or a problem too hard for him to solve or a request too big for him to answer. God does things no one else can do. And he does it over and above anything you could ever hope or dream of. Don't struggle trying to do things by the "arm of the flesh" when you have an omnipotent God ready and willing to help. *"You have not because you ask not."*

DAY 252   September 9

IF YOU HONESTLY trust God with all your heart and have given your life to him, you can positively know that anything that happens in your life is allowed by him. It does not matter how it seems or looks, God is sovereign in your life and has control over everything. Embrace your circumstances as part of the grand scheme for your life. Everything WILL work toward good if you are trusting God.

FOLLOW YOUR HEART! If there is a choice between following your heart or your head, always go with your heart. Use your head to determine if a motive is right, but if what is in your heart has the right motive, then extravagantly follow after it, and do not allow your head or critics to steal your vision.

DAY 253   September 10

YOUR FEAR OF displeasing other people puts you in bondage to them, and they become your primary focus. If you will spend your days trying to please God instead of man, everything else will fall into place and you will have favor with God and man. While it is a godly characteristic to consider others more important than yourself, be careful not to put man in a place of idolatry. Only God should get that elevated position.

MOST OF THE shadows in our lives are caused because we stand in our own sunshine. Many times we block our own blessings by stepping out of the protective boundaries that God has set. God has a code of ethics that are instilled in every human. "Choose" to live by them, and all other things will be added.

DAY 254   September 11

WE ARE LIVING in a time when everything is "instant." We not only want it right now, we can have it right now. Impatience has become a way of life and yet God's Word says that patience produces hope and strength and causes us to rise up with wings like eagles. Be still and know that He is God! *"Grow not weary of well doing, in due season you shall have your reward."*

WHAT WE ACTUALLY do shows what we really believe. We can say we believe all we want, but if we are not living it and putting action to it, it has no value. If we say that we believe God's Word, but don't do what he tells us to do, we are fooling ourselves. God gives us specific instructions on every single issue of life. If we really believe his Word, we will be doing life his way.

DAY 255   September 12

YOUR DNA IS unique, and so is your legacy. Your legacy is a compilation of every word, every action—everything you have ever done. It is all woven into the tapestry that makes up your life. Your legacy is an echo that continues even to the tenth generation. Leave those that follow you an echo of beauty, self-worth, dignity, and godliness. Your life does matter, and it's not how you start, but how you finish!

DON'T NEGATE THE importance of a "gut feeling." It has been proven that the gut feeling is usually the right choice. It has nothing to do with the intellect. In fact, the intellect can cause us to make choices that are not from God. When everything seems right, but there is a little nagging feeling in your gut, pay attention. It is probably God directing your steps, just as he promises.

DAY 256   September 13

WE HAVE THE power to make our choices, but our choices have the power to make or break us. There is much talk about the right to choose—and God gives us that—but your choice has the power to either destroy you or make you successful. Always choose what you instinctively know is the "right" choice. The whole of our life becomes a tapestry of every choice we've ever made. Choose well!

KIND, THANKFUL PEOPLE have been found to be less stressed and live healthier, happier lives. When we choose to live by God's standards, there comes with it a sense of well being that lifts burdens and brings joy. Doing the right thing always pays off in the end.

Day 257   September 14

A PERSON LIVING for others can and often does make a difference. God uses humans to fulfill his plans; be aware of what is going on around you and allow God to use you to impact others. Share with and help others, even if it means stepping out of your comfort zone. *"Whatever good thing you do for others, God will do for you."*

IF YOU DON'T make good choices today, you will have regrets tomorrow. Every choice we make is a seed sown, and every seed sown will produce some sort of harvest, whether thistles and thorns or beautiful, juicy fruit. Nothing impacts our life more than the choices we make. *"I lay before you life and death, blessing and cursing...choose life."* Your choice!

Day 258   September 15

THE PURPOSE OF prayer is not to bend God to our will, but to align ourselves to his will as we pray. His Word says that he will *"work in us to will and to do his good pleasure."* So if we are submitted to God, we will have a desire to do what he wants us to do. This, of course, does not include anything that goes against his Word, including carnal fleshly desires. Give attention to those desires that are within you. If you are really seeking God, it is probably him gently nudging you toward his plan for you. He promises his servants that he will give them the desires of their heart. I like that!

THE WORD SAYS, *"Money quickly gotten is quickly lost, but amassed little by little it has great value."* This is true about everything in life; if you have a little and you love it and work it, and you are faithful with it, I promise you it will one day turn into something very valuable, and you will have a deeper appreciation of it than if it had been handed to you. God tells us to not despise small beginnings. If you will simply take what you have been given and plug along at a steady pace, in due season it will succeed!

Day 259   September 16

SEEK OUT AND spend time with those who celebrate you, instead of those who only "tolerate" you. Friends have a huge impact on our confidence level. God celebrates everything about you. Be a God-pleaser rather than a man-pleaser and your friendships will fall into line.

WHEN YOU HAVE a situation in your life that is troubling, instead of fretting, ask yourself, *What is more true: your situation, or what God says about your situation?*, *"As you believe, it is done unto you."* Be determined to believe what God says. It's not always easy but it can be done. Don't be moved by what you see with your eyes. We are to *"walk by faith, not by sight,"* and *"blessed are those who have never seen but still believe."*

DAY 260 September 17

HONOR YOUR MOTHER and your father that it may go well with you and you will live long in the land. It does not say, "Unless they were not a good parent, or unless they did something you didn't like." We are called to honor our parents! Even though many parents have seriously harmed their children, we are still called to honor them. I think it would behoove all of us to research the word *honor*. If we are not honoring our parents in the manner that we have been called, it will not go well for us.

PAYING IT FORWARD is doing something unexpectedly good for someone because someone else did that for you. Find someone today who needs encouraging and bless them with a word, a touch, a good deed, and maybe even a present or a few bucks. Let God use you to bless others and he will bless you.

DAY 261   September 18

NEVER THINK THAT God isn't big enough to handle your problems. We can't even begin to imagine what God is capable of. We serve a big God! He is not too busy. I have actually heard people say things like "God has better things to do than to help me with my problems." He is not limited to doing one thing at a time; he can do everything at once. Expect him to do big things in your life. Remember, *"as a man believes, so he is."* Believe big!

WHEN A PERSON is really living for God, their value system will change. Truth will not be elusive to them because *"they know the truth and the truth will set them free."* They will be able to discern right from wrong and they will have a love and a kindred connection to the brethren. There will be a recognizable *"peace that goes beyond understanding"* in their life. "Believing" in God and "living" for God are not the same thing. Believing is only the beginning of wisdom, while living for and serving God is an honor and blessing that goes beyond description.

DAY 262   September 19

LITTLE "WHITE LIES" are still lies, and God's Word says that Satan is the Father of Lies. It is not okay to lie! When you tell a fib, no matter how small the fib may be, it will come back on you, and you usually have to tell another whopper to protect yourself from the first one. Lies represent a lack of integrity and are indicative of one whose moral compass has run amok. Honesty is truly the best policy—stick with the truth or keep your mouth shut.

LIFE IS NOT about what you have, it's about what you do with what you have. Do something great with your life! Whatever you have been given to do, do it with all your might. Every detail in your life will increase when you give things your all. Purpose in your heart to be successful!

Day 263   September 20

TAKE TIME TO encourage others. Don't get so busy looking at yourself that you become insensitive to the needs of others. You never know when a loving word from you could change or even save a life. Be generous with kind words!

LET GOD USE you to infuse joy into others. We actually have the ability to make others happy, and we also have the ability to make ourselves happy. Do not allow yourself to get down into the sorrows of life or fret over the things that are going wrong. Nothing is permanent, and things can change for the better as quickly as they changed for the worse. Stir up the joy that is within you, and celebrate your days.

DAY 264   September 21

"AS IRON SHARPENS iron, so the countenance of a friend sharpens a friend." The value of true friends cannot be measured, and those who have friends must *"show themselves friendly."* The only kind of friendship you will ever have is the kind of friendship you are willing to give to others.

BE SELECTIVE ABOUT sharing your dream with just anyone. Share your dreams with trusted, like-minded people, because people can actually frustrate and waylay your plans. The nature of fallen man does not always want to see others succeed and can actually sabotage your success with negativity. Stay passionate about your dream and remember that God-given dreams will never manifest without faith.

DAY 265 September 22

WE NEED TO take responsibility for our own health. While doctors are sometimes necessary, we should not be looking to them to make our health decisions. God made our bodies wondrously, and if we choose to take care of them, they are capable of healing themselves. Our part is to help them by feeding them well. What you eat is either your medicine or your poison. Choose well; your life depends on it!

IF YOU TRY to do things that God has not called you to do, it will almost always fail—and it will not make you happy. Unhappiness is usually caused by wanting what you don't have, envying others, and being ungrateful for what God has given you. God blesses and protects those things that he has given you to do. There is such a freedom in being who God created you to be.

DAY 266   September 23

THE LOSS OF a loved one is devastating. It might feel for a time like your heart will break, but life still goes on and the hole that is left in your heart will eventually be filled. There is a natural time of grief that must be walked out, as you gently move the lost loved one into a small corner of your heart to make room for what God has for your future. Trust God and be willing to *"forget those things that are behind and look toward those things that are ahead."*

DON'T JUDGE YOURSELF by past mistakes. Release yourself from the past and do not define your future by things that have happened to you, or the guilt you feel because of things you have done. If you have asked God for forgiveness, "he does not even remember your sin anymore." It is unproductive and unhealthy to hang on to regrets. "God is faithful to finish the good work he has started in you." Every morning begins with a clean slate on which you can write whatever you choose.

THE WAY WE respond to adversity will define our character. There will always be times in our life that we will have to deal with adversity. None of us will escape, and our reaction to that adversity will tell a lot about us. In times of adversity, be proactive without being over-reactive. Get busy and do something productive to correct the situation instead of getting panicky and overly excitable. My immediate response is a quick prayer and then I take action, trusting God and knowing that he will direct my steps just as he promises.

THERE ARE TIMES when words do not have to be eloquent; we can simply tell someone that everything is going to be okay and that they are going to be okay. That can actually be enough to set them on the road of recovery. Those words can bring hope and courage. Be generous with comforting words. *"A word fitly spoken is like apples of gold in settings of silver."*

Day 268   September 25

IT IS WONDERFUL to have "potential," but without perseverance and determination it is about as useful as a withered hand. God gives the gifts, but we have to activate them by applying our own energy. Don't be discouraged or intimidated by a "little potential." If it is well worked, it will win the race over those who have tons of potential but don't act on it.

PRAYERS DO NOT have to be eloquent. In fact, sometimes the simple prayer is best. God knows your needs even before you ask, but for some reason he still tells us to ask. He says, *"You have not because you ask not."* Many times I simply call out a person's name, and God knows the rest. There are also times I pour my heart out to God. When you pray, whether it's lengthy or simple, rest assured God hears!

DAY 269   September 26

PRAYER IS A dialog between you and God. It is not just a monologue where you do all the talking. Listen for God's voice. He speaks through the Bible, through others, or through a small, gentle urging that comes from within. He can use many ways to communicate. If you will stop and listen, you will hear his voice.

WE ALL WORRY way too much about what other people think about us, when we should be more concerned about what God thinks about us. When we strive to please God, we fully develop the person we were created to be. We do not have to compete with others; God made each of us unique. Max out your own individual character.

DAY 270   September 27

YOU CAN'T KEEP pain out of your life forever. Life can change in a moment's time, so savor the moments of joy and be encouraged that when sorrow is with you, joy is asleep upon your bed. When things are painful, remember that "this too shall pass."

WHEN YOU CAN'T figure out what to do, or when there are too many choices, it is best to do nothing and just walk out the situation. God promises to direct our steps, and sometimes we strive so hard trying to make decisions, we miss the peaceful move of God in our life. Remember that the wisdom from above is *"first pure and then peaceful."* If is not peaceful, it is not God.

DAY 271   September 28

MANY TIMES WHEN we make a commitment and decide to serve God in a particular situation, everything goes awry. God's Word will actually try us, but if you trust God and do what is right, God will enrich your life. It is so easy to fall into the way the world does it, but always do what is right. It is so satisfying when you follow God's Word and will always pay off. You know what is right; just do it!

THE WORDS *THANK you, forgive me, I was wrong*, and *excuse me* are powerful tools for a happy life. It is a beautiful strength to be able to admit your faults and errors. As children we would quickly defend our position no matter how wrong we were, but as adults we should always be fair in our analysis of a problem. If you have a problem with someone and you can simply say, "For whatever part I played in this problem, I am truly sorry. What can I do to make things better?" most problems will resolve. Consider others more important than yourself.

DAY 272   September 29

IT IS EXCITING and fun to serve God. It opens your life to miracles! Furthermore, when you are serving God, you will be making good choices, and good choices just make life sweeter. Life is never boring; there is always an element of excitement and anticipation of what God might do next.

MARRIAGE IS A lifelong journey that left unattended becomes much like a plant in the ground that is not fed or watered. Way too many marriages are "ho-hum." They take their love for granted and it has stopped growing and moving and going deeper. They muddle through life together, barely speaking to one another and without any real excitement. Perfected love is possible but it always requires diligence. Tend your marriage properly and watch it blossom. *"When a man finds a wife, he finds a good thing."* Marriage, even though hard at times, should always be good.

DAY 273   September 30

THE WORDS *I promise* are not in the Bible, even though the Word contains thousands of promises. This is because if God says it, it is true and he does not need to make any more proclamations about what he has promised. He tells us to *"bring him in remembrance of his word,"* not because he does not know what he says, but he wants to know that we know. Search out these precious hidden treasures that can literally cover every situation in your life, and then believe that they belong to you, remembering that *"as you believe, it is done unto you."*

EVEN THOUGH OUR pathways twist and turn through stony landscapes, if we look back, we will see thousands of miles of miracles and answered prayers. Life is full of potholes and bumps in the road; travel your journey with a confidence that our God goes with you and will see you through every mishap. Watch for the little signs of his presence in your life. It is usually in the little things wherein his miracles lie.

October

OUR WORDS HAVE the power to impact others for a lifetime. They can be apologized for and forgiven, but once they are out there, they cannot be retrieved. Words can destroy a relationship, even a life. Be intentional with your words, especially with young people. You can make or break a young person with what you tell them about themselves. The power of life and death is in the tongue. Use this powerful weapon to bless, not curse, yourself and others.

GOD TELLS US not to lean on our own understanding but to put our trust in him, and he will make our paths straight. Yet most of the time we try to analyze everything and figure it out for ourselves. Let's start doing what God says, acknowledging him in all our ways, and trusting that he will make our paths straight as we put our best foot forward and walk out this journey.

GOD DOES NOT see one sin as worse than the other. People make the assumption that some sins are worse than others, and this is not so. Sin is sin in God's eyes, and he will forgive any sin if we ask for forgiveness and turns from our ways. If God will forgive even heinous sins, then we should be willing to forgive others also. God says to *"take the board out of your own eye before you try to take the speck out of your brother's eye."* Only God has the right to judge.

GOD WORKS OUR hearts to move us in the direction he wants us to go. Sometimes it may seem that we are bumbling through life without much direction, but if we really trust God, he has pointed us to go a certain way. Don't feel discouraged when you look at your surroundings. God has a plan if you are trusting him. Many times we have to journey through the wilderness before we get to the promised land.

DAY 276   October 3

HOLDING GRUDGES AGAINST people will make you sick. It doesn't matter that you can rationalize why you are holding the grudge. God does not give us any excuses for unforgiveness. It doesn't matter if it is an ex-wife or ex-husband, or children that were conceived from a previous marriage, or a relative that has wronged you, or even a political figure you don't agree with. Unforgiveness and haughtiness will bring you down. *"As you forgive, you are forgiven."*

IF YOU THINK you can, you can. If you think you can't, you can't. Never allow yourself to doubt your abilities. Negative thoughts bring negative results. *"We can do all things through Christ who strengthens us."* Ask God for help in everything and then proceed, knowing you *can* do it!

Day 277   October 4

BEING AN IMPROVISER is being a problem solver. And problem solving is the key to our worldly success. God tells us to be good stewards with what we have, and improvising is part of that stewardship. "Where there's a will there's a way." Find the way and get things done where you are, with what you have.

ACTING SILLY AND ridiculous brings a special kind of *happy*! Life is full of serious moments, and it is so important to have those people in your life with whom you let down all facades and howl with laughter. *"A merry heart does good like a medicine."* Have fun!

DAY 278   October 5

SELF-PITY IS ALWAYS accompanied by negative thoughts—what you don't have, people who don't love you, all the work you have to do, all the problems you have. All of these are rooted in self-pity and are tools of manipulation. You cannot be pitiful and powerful at the same time. We all have cause for self-pity if that is what we choose to focus on. I choose to believe that *"I can do all things through Christ who strengthens me."*

WHEN WE DO what is right, there will be peace, and *"the effect of doing what is right brings quietness and assurance."* Don't you just love that! We are all looking for peace and assurance, and it is simply doing what is right by honoring God. Remember that God's promises are real. Find them, believe them, and act on them. Do not be moved by your circumstances— they are temporary. *"Delight yourself in the Lord and he will give you the desires of your heart."*

DAY 279   October 6

WHEN YOU ARE well maintained on the outside, it seems to seep in. God says that his people are the temple of the Holy Spirit, and therefore we should maintain our temple in a presentable way. It would be out of order to see a church that needed painting, with broken windows and an unchecked yard. Likewise, we should keep ourselves well maintained. I believe that every Christian should look their best at all times, not because of vanity but because we represent our Father in heaven. You'll find that when you look good, you feel good. Always do your best with what you have to work with.

THERE IS A lot more to life than where you are now. There are more things to do than what you've already done. Purpose to meet new people, go to new places, and believe you can do it. If you don't believe you can do it, you won't be able to. Ask God to show you the hidden treasures in secret places, and also ask him to give you the strength and courage you need to move your life forward.

UNFORGIVENESS WILL MAKE you sick and actually prevent healing. There is no denying that it can be extremely difficult to forgive those who have deeply wronged us, but unforgiveness is an acid that eats the vessel that holds it. Ask God to help you to forgive and then do what you can to perpetrate a mutual healing. *"If it be possible, as much as lies within you, be at peace with all men."*

KEEP YOURSELF AWAY from the confines of self-righteous authority as much as possible. There are situations where this type of authority cannot be avoided, but when possible stay clear of these individuals who cause feelings of guilt, insecurities, and unworthiness as they abuse their authority over others with unnecessary roughness. God never uses this sort of degrading correction, so reject it even if it is given in the name of the Lord.

DAY 281   October 8

DON'T GIVE UP just because you didn't succeed the first time. Find another way to do things. Go around the back door, jump over the hurdle, and push through. Don't assume that because there are roadblocks that God is trying to stop you. Don't worry, if God doesn't want you to have something, you will not be able to get over it, under it, around it, or through it. Your job is to try all of those possibilities. Success comes to those who are willing to push through. Trust as you go forward that God will direct your path. Expect to win!

PLAYING IT SAFE will get you nowhere. Be courageous! Step out and take chances. Boredom is the reward for no guts. *"Fear not and be of good courage."* Fear will neutralize your life and steal your zest for living, and you will end up with a boring life lived in a small box. Even small risks can change a life. Face the giant, even if you're scared. God goes with you.

YOUR JOY OR the lack thereof is connected to what you say. We use thousands of words a day and most of them are useless chatter. The more you chatter about your problems, the more problems you're going to have. Our words can cause us, and others, to succeed or fail. Be careful not to spew deadly "word bullets" out of your mouth. Spoken words cannot be retrieved and can set your life on a course of destruction.

PEOPLE OFTEN FEEL inadequate to pray out loud in front of others. They feel they are not capable of praying an eloquent prayer that will be acceptable to both God and man. But the truth is many times prayers are spoken with many words that are totally unnecessary. God already knows the needs, and our plethora of words are often used to impress others. There are two basic prayers that I think pretty much cover it all and are two of the most powerful prayers you will ever pray: "Help me" and "Thank you."

Day 283   October 10

PAY ATTENTION TO the hardships and the victories in your life; they are both equally as important to position you for the success of your spiritual and physical growth. The places that you experience successes and failures will determine the strength and the outcome of your future. *"Count it all joy as you go through the fiery trials, for they are perfecting you."*

READING, LISTENING, OR even memorizing God's Word does no good unless you implement it. I am amazed and grieved at how many people I see who call themselves Christians and yet judge and look down their noses at others, thinking of themselves more highly than they ought. God is the final judge of all of us, and as you judge, you will be judged. We are told to simply love others. It is God's battle, not yours.

DAY 284   October 11

GOD HAS A plan and a promise to restore whatever we have lost. God promises to *"restore the years the cankerworms have eaten."* Sometimes we are so busy fretting over what we have lost that we neglect to see what he has restored back to us in a different form. Take a moment and encourage yourself by looking back on your life and recognizing that everything that was lost has been replaced, and then give praise to God.

WHEN THE STUDENT is ready, the teacher will appear. We can hear truth over and over but until we are ready to receive it, it will not sink in. Truth is truth whether we believe it or not, but until we have ears to hear, it has no value for us. Ask God to open your heart and ears so that you may be able to hear the truth and activate its power in your life.

Day 285   October 12

GOD SAYS THAT he will use the weak things of this world to confound the wise. Never believe that just because you are not beautiful, rich, or come from a pedigree bloodline that God will not use you. It is only your doubt and your resistance that will prevent God from catapulting you upward. In fact, the more lowly and humble you consider yourself, the more likely that God has a big plan for your life. Remember that he loves to confound the wise.

DON'T BE AFRAID that God will not come through for you. He has a plan. Fear is the fundamental barrier to peace. Real peace has nothing to do with what's going on around you. The peace that the world offers is the lack of violence, while the peace that Jesus offers is in the midst of violence. Accept the fact that you will see all sorts of junk in the world, but God promises that it will not come near you. Hang on to that no matter what you see with your eyes.

DAY 286   October 13

WHEN WE DEMONSTRATE faith in God, it will weaken the powers of darkness that surround us. Darkness cannot be where there is light, and even one small candle lit in a dark room will bring light to the whole room. Always put light on everything and it will dispel the evil, ugly things. God's Word is a light upon your path.

MAKE DECISIONS AHEAD of time about how you will handle any given situation. Decide that you are always going to make the best of everything. Nothing is without some sort of annoyance, but your decision to "change what you can and accept what you can't" is a slogan we should all live by.

DAY 287   October 14

IT IS TEMPTING to give up when things don't seem to be working, yet God says to *"grow not weary of well doing, because in due season you will have your reward."* God tells us to bring him in remembrance of his word, so it is good to remind God of the promises he has given us. They are like hidden treasures within the pages of God's Word, and you have to dig them out yourself.

"BE NOT DECEIVED, *bad company corrupts good behavior."* Take a good look at your close friends because they will usually exemplify you. It is true that "water seeks its own level" and that "like attracts like." There is nothing wrong with short encounters with unsavory characters. Love them and be sweet to them as Jesus was, but spend the bulk of your time with those whom you want to be like, because eventually you will be.

DAY 288   October 15

DENIAL IS AN impediment to spiritual growth. Denying your weakness or your situation is not productive in any way. Although it is important not to profess negative things over and over, it is necessary to face reality. Assess your situation and ask God to help you with it, then begin to confess things that are not as though they are as you trust God for the answers.

WHAT YOU THINK, say, see, walk, and do will establish your life. Take charge of your thoughts, watch what comes out of your mouth, and walk with intentionality. Fix your gaze on whatever is lovely, beautiful, praiseworthy, and noble. There are always choices that must be made. God will guide you and establish your way, but you must make the decision to do your part. He will provide, but you must receive.

DAY 289   October 16

HARD WORK WILL always pay off! God promises that *"he will bless the work of your hands."* If you are willing to remain steadfast and wait for God's timing, you will be blessed in due season. But remember that the words of your mouth can actually negate the work of your hands. Busy hands and positive words are a dynamite duo!

WHEN WE CHOOSE to play the "victim" role in life, we will never be victorious. It is our choice. God did not make us that way. Playing the victim is nothing more than the downside of pride, and pride always comes before a fall. The downside of pride plays the pitiful, poor-me role and will never admit their part in a problem. They only see their side, and in the end they shoot themselves in the foot and limp away whining as they sulk and lick their self-inflicted wounds. What an ugly character flaw. Victim or victorious? Your choice!

Day 290   October 17

"THE WISDOM FROM above is first pure and then peaceful." God's direction is always pure, respectful, kind, gentle, honest, and considerate. It will never urge you to sin in any way. God's wisdom will also bring a calming peace that gives a feeling of "this is right." Always wait for this coveted feeling before making life-changing decisions. *"God works in us to will and to do his good pleasure."*

WALK OUT YOUR life with a confidence that no matter what happens, it will work toward good. Many times this is very difficult in the light of something horrible that is going on in your life, but if you can just get yourself to that place of faith that truly trusts God's Word, you will receive that peace that we are all looking for—the peace that goes beyond understanding. God is sovereign, and he can choose to "zap" something anytime he wants. If he doesn't, there is a purpose for it.

DAY 291   October 18

FEAR ACTIVATES THE enemy, while faith activates God. Fear is learned behavior. If we can learn it, we can unlearn it. Fear is a thief of life. I know this sounds simple, but God says, *"Call on to me and I will deliver you from all of your fears."* It may not happen overnight, but little by little it will take hold. This is God's promise to his children. *"Has he said it, and will he not do it?"*

IF YOU DON'T look for God or listen for God, you won't see or hear him. When good things happen, you will call it a coincidence or good luck. *"If you draw close to God, he will draw close to you."* Seek him and then expect his promises to be fulfilled in your life. And remember to stop and say thank you. God loves everyone the same, but he does show favor to those who look to him and are grateful. God's favor shining down on you is the best gift you could ever receive.

LIFE CAN ONLY be understood backward, but it must be lived forward. This is just the way it is. Every life happening gives us the opportunity to blaze a trail for those coming up behind us. Live your life forward, as you glean from those who go before you. *"A wise man learns by watching."*

DO NOT ALLOW yourself to be defeated because of the wrong choices that were made in the past, and don't let past decisions define who you are in the present. We all have seasons in life that we did not do things exactly right. Don't beat yourself up over past mistakes, and don't receive guilt that others may try to put on you because of something you did in the past. Simply use past mistakes as a compass to guide you where you do not want to go again. It's not how you start that counts, but how you finish.

DAY 293   October 20

BE DECISIVE, RIGHT or wrong, but make a decision. Things need to be done. It is good to take time to think things through rather than make an impulsive decision, but the old adage "He who hesitates is lost" has validity. Sometimes we overthink things, and the longer we take to make a decision, the more complicated things get. Sometimes the first instinct is actually the best. God directs our steps, so keep the steps moving and expect his direction to guide you.

WE ALL KNOW that *"pride comes before a fall,"* but we don't hear or pay much attention to the rest of that proverb—"and a haughty spirit before destruction." Don't allow yourself to operate in this attitude that can take you down. Always be mindful of how you treat people. This is a powerful proverb!

DAY 294   October 21

THE TRUE ANSWER for anxiety issues is spiritual. If we learn to meditate on God's goodness and ponder his power and promises, we can find peace. *"You will keep him in perfect peace whose mind is stayed on you."* We are all seeking peace and, while there are lots of generic remedies in the world, the truth is that only God can give the peace that goes beyond understanding.

IT IS TRUE that "hurt people hurt people." When Jesus looked at the crowd of people who eventually hung him on a cross, the Bible says that he was moved with compassion. If we can just remember that people have been through tremendous things themselves that have caused them to react in a negative way toward others, it will help us to be moved with compassion. It is very difficult to be angry with someone you have compassion for. I personally think compassion and mercy are the real keys to forgiveness. *"Those who show mercy will themselves receive mercy."*

DAY 295   October 22

MANY TIMES PEOPLE attach themselves to hurtful people or harmful situations because they want to escape being alone. God promises to never leave us or forsake us. Attach yourself to God and find the comfort that every human longs for. People are wonderful but they will never fulfill all your needs; only God can do that.

IF YOU WANT to slay the giants in your life, you have to be disciplined. The enemies in your life will always show up at your lowest point, and as long as you stay down, the giants will always look bigger; they love to kick you when you're down. Get up and face your giants, and they will seem smaller! You never get victory in your life if you cower in a corner and don't speak up. The key is to ask God for wisdom and favor and then come out swinging. *"If God be for you, who can be against you?"*

DAY 296   October 23

ALL THINGS DONE in the dark will eventually come to light. Sometimes we think we are pulling something off by being dishonest or covering things up, but in the end everything will be exposed. Honesty is truly the best policy. While sometimes it is best not to say anything if you can't say something nice, if you do say something, make sure it is the truth or it will come back to bite you.

"DELIGHT YOURSELF IN the Lord and he will give you the desires of your heart." We all want the desires of our heart, and this is actually God's promise to those who seek to do his will and spend time getting to know him. What a wonderful promise! You can't do things your way and expect God's Word to work in your life. Delight yourself in him and watch what he will do with your mundane world.

DAY 297 October 24

"TWO PASSIONS BEAT within my chest, the one is foul, the other blessed. The one I love, the other I hate; the one I feed will dominate."[2][[Jerry, footnote: [2]Unknown author.]] Whatever passion you are feeding in your life will be what grows. Don't feed yourself gossip, horror movies, or negative news. Feed your faith with God's Word and you can handle anything.

THE STORMS OF life are not an option, but fear is. Storms will always come, but fear becomes a choice. When doubts come and the storms are raging, exercise your faith. Remember that fear cannot be where there is faith. It is like putting a candle in a dark room and expecting the room to stay dark. Faith is the light that dispels fear. *"Darkness cannot be where there is light."*

THE WISDOM FROM above is first pure and then peaceful. How many times have we wondered, *Is that you, God?* This verse tells us how to know. First, it must be pure and noble, not hurtful to anyone, and it cannot conflict with God's Word in any way, even if it is socially acceptable. Second, you must feel a peace about your decision. As the old saying goes, "When in doubt, back out." Doubt is not peaceful. If you trust God in the simplicity of his direction, you will not make a mistake. *"God will work all things toward good."*

WALK OUT YOUR life with an attitude of celebration. Wandering around with your head down and sighing because life is so tough will get you nowhere and will actually alienate you from others. No one likes to be around someone who is always down and whining about life. We all have our problems. No one is spared problems in this life, but it is your choice how you will handle them. Walk lightly with your head held high and a spring in your step, even if you have to "fake it till you make it."

DAY 299   October 26

A TIMELY WORD is delightful. There are times that the simplicity of helping someone is just a kind word. I love the word *delightful*, which means, "giving great pleasure." This is what God calls a word given in due season to someone who needs to hear that very thing. Make a sincere effort to help others with a timely word. You do not have to be phony; simply choose to say the sweet things that you see or feel. If you see something nice, or pretty, or noble, just say it! Never keep good thoughts about others to yourself. They are apples of gold and can actually change lives!

IF YOU EXPECT nothing from God, that's what you'll get every time. *"As you believe, it is done unto you."* Our admission of an omnipotent God is only *"the beginning of wisdom."* All the education in the world does not make a person wise; in fact, God tells us *"the wisdom of this world is foolishness to him."* No matter how smart or educated a person is, they are never smart enough to get by without God. They will eventually find themselves in a foxhole. Money, books, computers, fame, people, education—all for naught. "Only one life will soon be past and only what's done for God will last."

GOD'S WORD SAYS that he will not allow the righteous to be moved. When you stop and ponder that statement, it is pretty profound. If you are standing and believing while your life seems to be going in every direction, trust that the path is being laid and he will not allow you to be moved off the course. Even if it seems like you are spinning your wheels, have faith and be encouraged; God's Word is true and it is not affected by your circumstances.

THERE IS NO winning in comparison. There will always be someone richer, prettier, thinner, or smarter than you. When you compare yourself to others, God's Word says that you will either become vain or insecure. We are all created uniquely and intricately and we all have our own special set of attributes that should never be compared to anyone else's. *"You are fearfully and wonderfully made."* Love who you are!

Day 301   October 28

WE CAN FIND joy in a broken world. The world is full of offenses, but we can choose not to be offended. Disrespect and lawlessness have become rampant all around us. Do not respond by trying to get even. We cannot play the part for others, but we can play our part in such a way that it sets a good example for others and we become part of the solution rather than part of the problem. Always choose to do what you know is right.

JESUS PLUS NOTHING equals everything. Many think they have been good and will therefore end up in heaven. This is called "works," and getting to heaven does not require works. Jesus died on the cross for our sins, and the simplicity of acknowledging him gets us to heaven. However, a sincere acknowledgement of Jesus will cause us to have good works. It just happens automatically. *"You will know them by their works."*

Day 302   October 29

SOMETIMES WE LOOK at those who have financial gain and think that they must have it all, that if we just had their money we would be happy. But the Word says, *"If God does not give the wealth, it will bring sorrow."* God knows our needs better than we do. Choose to be content with your lot in life, work hard at tending your garden, and know that God has a plan. It is a good plan to prosper you in the way that only God knows is best for you. True prosperity is not measured in money, but in a combination of many things that money can't buy.

WORDS ARE NOT always the culprit in misunderstandings. Be aware that you are putting out a body language or facial expression that many times speaks louder than words. The issues of life flow from the heart of man. Set your heart on the things that are pure and lovely and clean and noble, and the body will always follow.

DAY 303   October 30

LOOK BEYOND TODAY; don't get so lost in the day that you can't picture your future. While it is important to "live" in the moment, it is foolish to ignore the consequences of the choices you make today. As you refine your future, gently remember your past. While your past does not define you, it has brought you to where you are now. Let the mistakes in your past serve as a learning curve as you go forward.

SOMETIMES WE SPEND so much time struggling with complexities that we miss the sweet simplicities of life. Notice and interact with the gentle things that are ever present—the sound of birds singing, the smell of flowers, the constant movement of the sky, the sweet taste of clean water. There is so much to thank God for!

Day 304   October 31

LOVE IS A verb—an action—it is way more than just words or feelings. While what you say and feel is important, it is not the sign of true love. Feelings can change from moment to moment, and if you are basing your love on feelings, you will have problems. True love is deciding that you will love someone through thick and thin; it is making a decision to stand by them no matter what. *"Love is patient, love is kind, it does not envy or boast, and it is not self-seeking. It does not get easily angered or hold a grudge. It always protects, hopes, trusts, and perseveres."*

LOVE CAN OFTEN cause pain, but this does not necessarily mean that a relationship is not from God. "No pain, no gain." True love that has depth often involves lots of trouble and some adjustments. Many times people are so quick to abandon a relationship because there are hard issues involved. True love will work through these issues and "the iron that has been through the fire is the strongest."

November

PUTTING YOUR HEAD in the sand will never help. Face the circumstances of life; do what you can, and give the rest to God. Choose to see the good in everything and believe that everything will be all right. This is a healthy, godly perspective on life as long as it doesn't wander over into procrastination and denial. *"A good man brings good things out of the good stored up in his heart."*

YOU WILL RISE by lifting up others. Everyone needs to be encouraged, and if you will encourage others, God will encourage you. He says, *"Whatever good thing we do for others, he will do for us."* It is only the fall of man that makes him feel the need to bring others down in order to make himself feel elevated. It is actually the reverse that works; if you will build others up, you will yourself be built up. You can't put perfume on others without getting some of the sweet fragrance on yourself.

Day 306   November 2

WHAT OR WHOM we worship will determine our behavior. The things that we love and adore will have a huge impact on what we will become in life. Be aware of the things to which you are giving your affections. Are they admirable? Would they please God? Are they productive and noble? Many objects of worship are actually a ball and chain and will actually imprison us. Set God as your main source of worship and all other things will be added unto you.

ONLY GOD CAN turn a "trial" into a triumph and a "victim" into a victory. He can take the messes in your life and turn them into a fabulous testimony! *"With God, all things are possible."* Our part is to trust and believe. There is a time and a season for everything. Your season will come if you do not give up. *"Only Believe!"*

Day 307   November 3

PAIN IS NOT relieved by running away from it or by sweeping it under a rug. It is relieved by facing reality and allowing yourself to experience the fullness of the sorrow and trusting that it will pass. It is choosing to experience the joys in life even while the pain is present. *"Weeping may tarry with the night, but joy will come in the morning."*

GOD DOES NOT call his people to a life of misery. Misery is usually caused by our own actions or the actions of others in our life. We live in a fallen world where problems abound, but the way in which we choose to handle the problems that are certain to come will make the difference between whether we live a life of victory or a life of misery. Make a decision today that you are going to look to God and trust his word to see you through this life with a victorious outcome.

DAY 308   November 4

TAKE HEED TO what you hear because these are the things that will come out of you. What you hear will profoundly affect your life. Be intentional about what you listen to, including music. Sad, sexy, or angry songs can and does affect our personality. Surround yourself with happy, upbeat, faith-filled words and people.

UNCONDITIONAL LOVE WILL cause people to blossom. When people are loved properly, they will have more confidence, be more successful, stay healthier, and their countenance will glow. It has been proven that orphan babies who are not held and loved are stunted physically, mentally, and emotionally. As adults we still respond the same way. A friend, a child, or your mate—love each other well. *"Faith, hope, love. But the greatest of these is love."*

DAY 309   November 5

TRUE STRENGTH IS hanging on when everyone else would have given up. It is so easy to quit, but the big blessings come to those who persevere. *"Grow not weary in well doing, because in due season you shall have your reward."* Press on, and enjoy the journey!

COMMITMENT IS THE key to success in every area of your life. We become what we are committed to. Prioritize your life by putting first things first. Put God at the helm and everything else will fall gently into the proper order.

Day 310   November 6

YOU CAN NEVER have something better until you let loose of what you have. You can whine all you want about your life, but until you are ready to let go, you will never be able to move on to bigger and better things. You cannot put something in a space where there is already something else. Let go and let God! *"Has he said it, and will he not do it?"*

WE LIVE IN a fallen world. You could get cancer. Your children could go off the deep end. You could lose your job. A loved one could fall ill. All of these things can happen to you even as a Christian, but if you can get one thing down into your heart and really believe it, you will see a happier ending. In times of disruption and turmoil, there is one scripture that every Christian needs to hang on to: *"All things work together for good to those that love God."* That is all you need to know. You don't have to know why or how, you just have to believe it!

DAY 311   November 7

FORGIVE OTHERS EVEN when you think they don't deserve it. When you hold unforgiveness, it has been proven that it will affect your body and cause you pain and all sorts of mental and physical disorders. There are those in your life who have really hurt you—and God knows your hurt—but if you ask him to help, he will put that forgiveness in your heart. Really, really receive this one; it is so important!

COMPASSION IS WHAT you feel, while kindness is what you do. Kindness has a major impact on people, and we are all in desperate need of kindness. You will leave a trace of yourself on every single person you come in contact with or touch in life. Be aware of what trace you are leaving. Shine your light in such a way that your legacy will live long after you're gone and impact the generations that come after you. *"The blessings and cursings continue even to the tenth generation."*

DAY 312   November 8

IT IS EASY to trust God when things are going well, but the true test of faith is how we respond during stormy weather. Life is filled with problems—many times we create them ourselves, or our loved ones create them—and some things are just out of our control. These are tests that will prove your faith and can actually strengthen it. Exercise your faith by reading the Word of God and using it. I promise you there will be lots of tragedies in your life, times you will need your faith to be strong. No one escapes these trials. Exercise your faith!.

IT IS IGNORANT to blame God for your problems and the problems in the world. God gave man the freedom of choice, and that choice has wreaked havoc in the world. People ask, "How can a good God allow these things to happen?" The only thing God "allows" is the right to choose. The consequences of those choices are the very things they blame God for. God is a good God! He lays before us life and death and he tells us to choose life.

DAY 313   November 9

THERE ARE MANY times throughout our lives that we will come to a fork in the road, a point at which we must choose a direction to take. Once you have made your choice, go forward boldly and do not waiver, wondering if you made the right choice. If God has another direction for you, he will fine-tune your course as you go. Those who waiver get nothing from God.

A SWEET, LOVING marriage does not just happen. It is about considering the other more important than yourself, and choosing to see the good in your mate. It's about laughing together and never bad-mouthing each other. It's about loyalty, carrying your share of the load, and as my sister says, "It's about learning to shut up!"

DON'T EXPECT OTHERS to fulfill something in you that only God can fulfill. These kinds of impossible expectations put way too much pressure on the people you're close to and will almost always cause a relationship to fail. Look to God for your deepest needs. It is very fulfilling to have wonderful relationships, but always keep God at the helm.

LIVE YOUR LIFE and legacy by choice rather than by chance. Take charge of your life! Sometimes you will just bumble into something wonderful, but overall your success or lack thereof is determined by your willingness to step in and take charge. Be intentional about the legacy you want to leave and then make the necessary changes in your life to make it happen.

DON'T SPEND YOUR life lamenting over the things that have been done wrong to you, or the wrongs in the world. There will always be things that are troubling, and where you put your focus is what will stand out. Let God's goodness and beauty wash over you as you shake off all bitterness and sadness and choose the joy that is set before you.

THERE IS A false kind of sorrow that is called "the sorrow of the world." True sorrow always brings about repentance or a turning around, a making of restitution. Many times sorrow is only displayed because a person has been found out, not because they are truly sorry. True sorrow will always prove itself by actions and not just words. *"You will know them by their works."* Choose to live your life in such a way that you do not have to be sorry for anything.

Day 316   November 12

"IF ONLY" IS a statement of doubt, guilt, grief, regret, and disappointment. Rid yourself of this destructive statement. We all have regrets, but what's done is done and it is a waste of time and energy to beat yourself up over what could have been. There are lots of things that happen in our life that are *not* part of God's plan, but he promises to use them to our advantage when we trust him. Learn from your mistakes and move on. *"Forget those things that are behind and reach forward to those things that are ahead."*

THE THREE MOST important things in your life are: your master, your mission, and your mate. Your choice of these three topics will establish your life for good or bad. God, of course, should be your master. Your mission should be a God-given vision that is noble, executed excellently and passionately. And lastly, your mate is whom you are yoked with, either lifting you up or dragging you down.

WHEN WE CONNECT ourselves to others, it is like a three-way plug. It creates power! Being in true agreement with people who care gives us an amazing ability to accomplish impossible things. Stay in close community with people, and believe together for God's best in each other's lives.

NO ONE DESERVES the blessings that someone else has earned. Wonderful blessings await those who work hard and appreciate their own lot in life. If we kill the goose to get the golden egg, everyone loses.

DAY 318   November 14

WHEN YOUR LIFE is in chaos and everything around you is crashing, upbeat, glib statements can almost seem cruel, but keep in mind that your circumstances do not change these facts: God is still on the throne, and "this too shall pass." Your problem is not bigger than God. Don't give in to the urge to succumb to the problem. If you have done all you know to do, stand and believe God. *"Those who put their trust in God will never be disappointed."*

FAITH IS LIKE a muscle that will grow stronger with use. Without exercise, it will become impotent. Don't expect to move the mountains in your life if you have not bothered to work your faith. A buff body is not nearly as important as buff faith!

DAY 319   November 15

GIVING IS ONE of God's "kingdom secrets." Whatever you give out will always come back to you in greater quantity than it was given. This goes for everything. Whether it is tangible stuff or your words or actions, absolutely everything you give will be given! Be intentional about what you choose to give. Be sure it is what you want coming back.

MOST OF THE time, the things we cannot change end up changing us. There are certain things in our life that just don't go away no matter how hard we pray. The best thing we can do is try to work with it. Just because something is ugly doesn't mean we can't choose to see some beauty in it. We are all dealing with something that we would like to be done with. Things are only as big as we make them.

DAY 320 November 16

WE ALL HAVE sorrows about things that were lost in our life, whether it's people, things, or even money. There is a promise in the Bible that says, *"God will restore the years the canker worms have eaten."* He tells us to bring him in remembrance of his Word, and if you believe God's Word and you are willing to trust him on this one, he will restore anything you have ever lost, and it will be more than enough.

ALWAYS COVET THE high calling of being known as a person of integrity. When integrity is attributed to you, it brings favor on you from both God and man. Scoundrels may prevail for a season, but the faithful, trustworthy person will always win out!

HUMANS HAVE A hard time believing in something if they cannot see it, touch it, or smell it. And yet God lives in this spiritual, unseen realm. The spirit realm is very real and can create havoc in our life if we do not acknowledge it. Just as we cannot see or grasp the wind, it is very surely there. Give God equal courtesy as the wind by just believing.

WITHOUT A DOUBT means "perfect faith." The kind of faith that brings about God's perfect plan for your life is one that never waivers, one that does not entertain doubt, and one that is committed to the belief that if God's Word says it, that's all there is to it. God's Word says, *"He who wavers gets nothing from God."* Refuse to allow people, things, or circumstances to move you off of what God's Word says about your situation. *"Only believe."*

CELEBRATE YOUR VICTORIES rather than grieving over your losses. Life is full of losses but it is also full of victories. Choose to celebrate even the smallest of victories. Grief is a part of life, and it is okay and even healthy to grieve, as long as you do not wallow in it. Every season of life offers new hopes, dreams, relationships, and even a whole new ambiance surrounding you. Flow with your season and make every effort to appreciate and enjoy it. *"In all things give thanks."*

WE ALL HAVE weak areas in our character, and if you choose to deny and protect your flaws, you will never grow or change. Character flaws are part of being human, but if you embrace them they will gain strength and cause relationship problems. Always be willing to admit your areas of weakness. Manage your character instead of rationalizing why you are "just that way." Do your part and let God finish the work he has started in you. It is a lifelong process.

MAKE A CHOICE to enjoy life even while you are working or doing things that may not be considered fun. Bring joy to others and don't let others rob your joy. It is not what you do in life, but who you become that matters. Strive to become a fun person who makes the best out of everything that life brings along. Life can be that coveted bowl of cherries! *"This is the day that the Lord has made. I will rejoice and be glad in it."*

ALWAYS DO WHAT you know to be right. Sometimes it seems hard, especially in a world where anything goes. But right living and integrity will always lead to a good life. The little things do matter. The compilation of all the little things in your life are what eventually form the big picture. Your life's legacy is a continuous flow of all the choices you have made and the things that you have done throughout your life.

DAY 324   November 20

WHEN GOD'S WORD says *"all things work together for good for those that love God and are called according to his purpose,"* it actually means *all* things! When you look back over your life, you will see that many of the things that have made you the happiest were brought about by something you thought was disastrous. Be encouraged, for *"in due season you shall have your reward."*

PROBLEM-SOLVING IS THE highest level of education a person can receive. A master's degree cannot compare to the gift of being able to solve problems. Life is full of problems, and it doesn't take a college education to work through them. Gifted with problem-solving skills, a person can shoot right to the top of life with little or no education. *"All good gifts are from above."* Ask God to bless you with this "good gift" of problem-solving skills and then do your part to put them to work in your life.

DAY 325   November 21

IT IS SAID that "it is better to die for a conviction than to live with a compromise," but I don't necessarily agree. I believe that compromise in everyday life is a beautiful attribute and helps relationships to flow along smoothly. The only time that compromise should not be considered is when it comes to the Word of God. The trivial aspects of this life are temporal and should be compromised as you walk through life with your loved ones. *"Consider others more important than yourself."*

THE WISE MAN learns from others. It is downright ignorant to think you know it all. No matter how old you become, there is always more to learn. Pride is at the root of a "know-it-all," and *"pride comes before a fall."* Negativity is usually the response when someone doesn't know the answer but doesn't want to admit it. Be open to glean wisdom from others and admit when you don't know something.

DAY 326   November 22

BE MINDFUL OF the influence that you can have on other people. We have the ability to change the ambiance wherever we go. Your words and your attitude can not only make or break your day, but it can make or break the day of all the others around you. Choose to be that person who is the life of the party and brings joy and excitement to their friends, family, and co-workers. It's all about choice!

LEARN NOT TO lean on your own understanding and be not wise in your own eyes. There are times that we think we have learned it all and we puff ourselves up with our own wisdom. Be aware that these are the times that God will allow you to be brought down. Always stay humble, and remember that *"God gives grace to the humble and resists the proud."* No matter how much you think you know, always be willing to listen and learn; you never know who might bring a divine revelation to you right from God's mouth to your ears."

DAY 327   November 23

IF YOU DON'T raise your expectations about yourself, you will never get any better; you will remain in the same place you have always been. While it is important to be realistic, you can raise the bar in small, reasonable increments that are reachable goals for your personal set of abilities. Always be a good sport when others outperform you, but run your race of life as if to win.

"DELIGHT YOURSELF IN the Lord and he will give you the desires of your heart." We are all looking to get our desires fulfilled, and God gives us the prescription in this scripture. If we spend our days loving God, trusting him, and trying to do what is right, seeking him and his righteousness first, *"all other things will be added,"* including the desires of our heart. The human heart cannot even imagine how wonderful things can be when they come from God. Grow not weary; the best is yet to come!

Day 328   November 24

NEVER, NEVER, NEVER make decisions based on pride. I believe that most of us have blocked a ton of blessings because we operated in pride. Pride will never get you anywhere. Even though it can appear to make you look good, it is really one of the ugliest personality traits we can operate in. The Word says *"pride comes before a fall."* Enough said!

GOD SAYS YOU will find his wisdom if you *"cry out for discernment and lift up your voice for understanding."* When you are in a quandary of what to do, try crying out to God. He promises if you ask and really seek him that he will show you what to do. The problem is that many times we don't believe it's God when we get the answer. We ask, but we don't really believe that we will receive. Many times the answer comes in a way that we least expect or is not what we want to hear, so we actually turn it away. The antidote for that is trust. If you have asked, believe you have received and proceed accordingly.

Day 329   November 25

WHEN YOU CHOOSE God, it does not mean that life will be perfect or that all problems will magically disappear. But God's favor—his love, grace, mercy, comfort, and provision—will be the dominant and permanent theme in your life with him at the helm. Life will always have its ups and downs, and God will walk you through absolutely everything that could ever happen. Nothing will be as bad when he is by your side. *"Weeping may endure for a night, but joy will come in the morning."*

HE WHO ENDURES wins! The race does not always go to the swiftest. Instead, it is the one left standing who wins. I am convinced that most failures are not because of lack of talent, finances, abilities, circumstances, or luck, but rather the lack of discipline that creates endurance. To win the race, you must keep running. And you must *"run as if to win"*!

Day 330   November 26

WHEN WE GIVE, it is like sowing a seed in the ground; we plant the seed and then we expect a harvest. But not every seed we plant will produce. If the seed is not planted in good, healthy soil and tended properly, it will wither and die before it produces. Be attentive to the promptings of God about where to plant your seeds, and they will always produce a bountiful harvest.

IN ALL THINGS give thanks. We live in a culture that has a sense of entitlement. I don't know about you, but when someone acts like I owe them something, I tighten up like a clam. I think God operates the same way. I believe that gratefulness is one of the keys to getting the windows of heaven opened up over you. Remember to give heartfelt thanks to the Giver of all good things.

DAY 331   November 27

YOU CANNOT HAVE power and be pitiful at the same time. Feeling sorry for yourself is always accompanied by negative thoughts, and negative thoughts will take you down every time. Self-pity is actually very selfish. We are told to consider others more important than ourselves, but it is dangerous to pull inside of yourself and lament over past and present negative happenings. A better choice is to think on positive, beautiful, praiseworthy, noble things that always abound in the midst of life.

LAUGHTER WILL LIFT your load and lighten your heart. Don't take life so seriously; it weighs heavy on you when you look at everything with a serious eye. Learn to laugh and try to see the humor in even the most severe situations. *"Laughter does good like a medicine."*

DAY 332   November 28

THE WORST ENEMY of enthusiasm is time. A God-given vision can take years to manifest, and many times people give up on their dream while they are waiting. If you waiver, you will get nothing from God. If you have a good, logical dream, that will benefit yourself and others, it is probably from God. Don't give up on it. Do what you can with what you have until the vision comes to pass.

GOD HAS A special plan for all of his children *"to prosper and be in good health,"* but our choices and actions can detour God's best, and even foil his plans. Slothfulness, unforgiveness, overindulgence, booze, drugs, etc., he will forgive when you repent and work all *"toward good,"* but you have to play your part to receive his best. He will never take away your right to choose. Choose well!

DAY 333   November 29

IF YOU LIVE for God, practice goodness, and always try to do the right thing, God will bring your vision to pass. You must maintain your vision and see it to fruition. Just as you would tend a garden that has not produced fruit yet, so it is with your vision; water it, weed it, keep it safe from predators, and don't dig up the seed to see if it has sprouted yet. After you've done all you know to do, wait expectantly on God. Things that have taken years to come to pass can suddenly be fulfilled. *"Has He said it, and will He not do it?"*

THERE ARE CERTAIN things in life that cannot be fixed because we live in a sinful world. Do the best you can to keep your space in order and don't fret over what's wrong in the world. God promises his children that we will only see the reward of the wicked with our eyes, but it will not come near us. Trust him with all your heart and enjoy your days.

DAY 334   November 30

WHEN YOU CHANGE your thinking, you change your belief. When you change your belief, you change your expectations. When you change your expectations, you change your attitude. When you change your attitude, you change your behavior. And when you change your behavior, you change your life.

SOMETIMES THERE IS a tendency to balk at change, but change is a part of successful growth. When we cling to the rock instead of flowing with the natural movement of life, we become unteachable. The happiest people are those who are able to experience the adventure of a well-rounded life. Consider God first, and then go with the flow!

December

WE ARE ALL given a little "life garden" to tend. Some gardens start pretty scrawny and some are even planted in a crack. When loved and tended well, even the scrawniest of gardens will produce a bountiful harvest. Our background and circumstances may influence who we are, but we are solely responsible for who we become!

REFUSE TO LET the important issues in life get crowded out by the things that are irrelevant. Don't get so busy doing "stuff" that you can't find time for interruptions. Some of life's greatest opportunities come packaged as perceived interruptions. Look for God's hand in everything—even the pitfalls and annoyances. He directs the steps of the righteous.

Day 336   December 2

THE FEARS OF the wicked will come upon them. So, who are the wicked? Webster's says it is a mental disregard for truth, honor, justice, virtue, and righteousness. When we choose to walk in these ways, we are opening up all kinds of doors that will bring trouble into our lives. Disregarding what God has ordained for man will actually bring a curse of fear upon us, while the book of Proverbs also says *"an undeserved curse has nowhere to light."* God does not curse us; we curse ourselves by our actions. Walk uprightly!

GOD'S THUMBPRINT IS everywhere we look. It is so evident in the flowers, trees, landscape, and solar system, but nothing more incredible than the human life. The intricacies of the human body are more than miraculous. It takes enormous faith to believe that this amazing human creation could evolve from a piece of slime. This is about as logical as throwing a bunch of junk into a junkyard and having it turn into an airplane.

DAY 337   December 3

"THE LORD IS my shepherd and I shall not want"
does not mean we will always get everything we
want. It means we will be happy and contented with
what we have. True blessing is not about "stuff," even
though it often includes material things. But what we
should strive for is to be content and grateful for our
lot in life. This is the true blessing of God.

HAPPINESS AND JOY are not the same. You can
buy happiness. Stuff, things, and people will bring
you happiness but it is all temporary. Joy is eternal; it
is the settled assurance that all is well no matter what
your circumstances are. Joy has peace attached to it.
Jesus said, *"My peace I leave to you, not like the world
can give but only like I can give."* Joy is not dependent
on what you have; it is only dependent on your trust
in God. Joy and peace are coveted treasures that come
from knowing God.

DAY 338   December 4

WHERE THERE IS hope there is faith, and where there is faith miracles can happen. Miracles usually happen to those who are looking for them. And they are almost impossible without faith. Although God can create a miracle for even an unbeliever, they are usually reserved for those who expect them. Never give up on receiving a miracle for what you are believing God to do, even if it seems impossible. God can do all things.

IT IS NEVER okay to be rude and disrespectful. Freedom of speech does not give anyone the right to spew poison out of their mouth. *"If you repay good for evil, evil will never depart from your house."* Slander is evil. Just because man allows slander and calls it "freedom of speech," does not make it right with God. He is the final judge whether you believe in him or not. *"Evil is called good and good is called evil."* Be careful who you choose to follow.

DAY 339   December 5

FEAR IS THE polar opposite of faith. And remember that faith is the only thing that really pleases God; it is the thing that activates all of God's promises. Fear cannot be where there is faith, and faith only comes by hearing the Word of God. Dealing with fear? Try reading the Bible.

WHILE OTHER PEOPLE can add to your joy, they cannot be the source of your joy. You need to own your own happiness. When you are happy with your God and yourself, you can bring joy to others. If you are looking to exterior things before you can be happy, you will always be disappointed. People will die or let you down, and "stuff" is temporal. But the joy that comes from knowing and loving who God made you to be will radiate outward and you will be able to give and receive love with a delightful depth.

DAY 340   December 6

"LO THE WINTER is past and the rain is gone, flowers are blooming on the earth and the time of singing birds has come." No matter what you are going through, God promises us that it will pass. He says, *"Weeping may endure for a night, but joy comes in the morning."* Take God at his Word and trust that the morning will bring the joy that you are looking for.

THERE IS NO wisdom, no understanding, or no counsel against the Lord. It doesn't matter if something is not politically correct, it doesn't matter what the celebrities think about a certain issue—anything that goes against God's Word will never prosper in the end. God's Word is the only real truth and anything that sounds like truth that is not in the Bible is actually just someone's opinion. There are many truths written by other people, but the basics were always derived from the Bible. Period.

Day 341   December 7

FAITH IS SOMETHING we live by, not something we just have. Even though we are all given a *"measure of faith"* at birth, many people never activate it by using it, and it stays a "baby faith" all their life. We must hear the Word of God to make it grow and then we must use it to build it up. Living by faith is a powerful choice that makes life so much easier, and more fun!

GOD DOES NOT use people who won't submit to authority. It is wonderful to be a leader, but all of us need to obey the authorities that have been placed over us. Obvious authorities are police officers, your boss, church leaders, and government. There is a rebellious lawlessness that permeates our country. Do not be part of that! God will never use people who come against the authorities that he has placed over us. *"God puts every authority in their place to accomplish his purposes."*

DAY 342   December 8

WE ALL HAVE ugly things in our past that just need to be forgotten. It is not necessary to remember and confess past mistakes over and over. If you have asked for forgiveness from God and done all you can to make restitution, then forget it and get on with life. You do not need to ever remember it again, because God says that not only are you forgiven but *"he doesn't even remember your sin anymore,"* so why should you?

PRIDE IS AN ugly character trait, and God says he hates it. Pride will stunt your growth, block your blessings, and make you fall. Never entertain pride, and never make any decisions based on pride. Sometimes when a person seems humble and pitiful, it is nothing more than pride operating in a reverse way. The person who needs help but takes offense when you offer it is operating in "low pride." Smother any urges to operate in any form of this destructive trait.

DAY 343   December 9

DO WHAT YOU can with what you have, right where you are. Not doing something because you think you need MORE will rob you of success. You will never have "enough" if you wait for everything to be perfect. Trust God as you battle the giants in your life and go for it!

GOD WORKS IN the hearts of people to move them in the direction he wants them to go, and sometimes it may seem that the brook has dried up. This is usually because God wants to move you on. It isn't profitable to dwell on and lament over why things have happened. The most productive thing is to pick up the pieces and mend things as best you can—or maybe even make a complete change in direction. God promises to direct the steps of the righteous, so don't curl up in a ball and give up. Keep moving, and eventually you'll find yourself in a fresh new space, prepared just for you. Just trust!

DAY 344   December 10

*"**THE POWER OF** life and death are in the tongue."*
Do not take your words lightly because eventually
you will get what you speak out. Even when we say
things in jest, the power of the tongue is still capable
of bringing things to pass. Choose words that bring
blessings on yourself and others.

A HAUGHTY SPIRIT will cause you to fall, and
pride will actually bring destruction. Many times we
wonder what happened. Everything has gone awry
and we can't figure it out. God gives us some pretty
clear reasons in his Word. Sometimes we are so dense
or we think we can disobey God's instructions and
still get by with it. We get into a pity party; we point
fingers at others and don't stop to find out what the
book of instructions says about our situation. And
worse yet, we don't even read the book of instruc-
tions and yet expect our life to run like a fine-tuned
Ferrari. At least read the book of Proverbs and get
God's "basic instructions."

DAY 345   December 11

OUR PAST IS a beautiful part of our history, and while it should be remembered fondly we should not sit around and romanticize all that has happened in the past. When we begin to move forward we activate God in our life. He promises to direct our steps toward the future, not our sitting around dreaming about yesteryear. God's Word has a promise that says, *"Your latter years will be better than your former years."* I'm laying hold of that one for myself!

GOD USES CONVICTION to reroute our life path when he sees us out of whack, but guilt is not the same as conviction, and it is not from God. Guilt will rob your joy and paralyze your growth! It is actually a form of unforgiveness toward yourself. We all make mistakes. A sincere apology wipes your slate clean with God, so forgive yourself and get on with life. No more guilt!

DAY 346   December 12

WE ARE ASSURED success if we stay within the spiritual perimeters that God has set for mankind. Every decision we make will either be one to assure our spiritual success or one that will follow the flesh—and the flesh will eventually lead us astray. The flesh knows no boundaries, it loves to overeat, it hates to exercise, and it loves all sorts of sensationalism. *"The spirit is strong, but the flesh is weak."* Let your spirit rule.

THINGS YOU BELIEVE deep down are what define you and cause you to react in certain ways. Take note of unplanned words that shoot out of your mouth or undeserved negative reactions toward people and things. These are reactions to suppressed, hidden feelings that are stuffed deep inside, and just because they are hidden does not mean they are benign. Darkness is toxic! It harbors fear and anxiety. Things are never as bad in the light as they seem in the dark. Expose the darkness, for *"darkness cannot be where there is light."*

Day 347   December 13

IT IS AMAZING to see what God can do with someone who will not give up. Oftentimes problems define our character and can either make us bitter or better. The easy way out of problems is to just quit, or sweep it under the rug and pretend it's not there. The better way is to accept the challenge that problems always present and get busy cleaning up the mess. God really does help those who help themselves!

A LIFE OF praise and thankfulness becomes a life filled with miracles! When we are grateful and thankful for what we have, everything looks prettier and the colors get brighter. This does not mean things are perfect; it means we have chosen to accept our lot in life and to tenderly care for it. It does not matter if your lot is small and unattractive. If you tend it properly, it will produce a beautiful lifetime harvest. *"The diligent hand shall rule."*

DAY 348   December 14

WHEN WE CHOOSE to give something up for God, he will always replace it with something better. Be willing to set aside the things in life that do not honor God, and then watch what happens. There will be a sweetness in your life that you have never experienced before. When God tells us not to do something, it is not for his benefit, but ours. Blessings will always follow obedience.

THE WRATH OF man will never accomplish the purposes of God. Getting mad about a situation that is already troubling will only make it worse. The wisdom of God is always peaceful. Passive-aggressive anger is not better. Huffing around and saying nothing's wrong is equally as damaging. Choose not to go there.

DAY 349   December 15

CONFUSION, DISTRESS, AND disease are not part of the inheritance that God left his people. However, we are subject to these things because we live in a fallen world. Our protection comes by staying under the umbrella that God has provided when we follow the rules. Sin causes us to step out from under the protective umbrella, and we become subject to all sorts of things. The laws of God are for our protection. Follow the rules!

WHEN YOU ARE worrying, you're are acting like you don't think God can handle things. Jesus tells us *not* to worry. This is not because what you are worried about is not important; it is because your worry is not fruitful. Giving it to God is the antidote to worry. *"Fret not, it will only cause harm."* Take a deep breath and say, "God knows my needs." *"Seek first the kingdom of God and his righteousness and all other things shall be added to you."*

DAY 350   December 16

CHAOS IN YOUR surroundings will make it hard to find peace within yourself. Our surroundings affect our thought processes, and it is up to us to keep those surroundings orderly and clean. While you cannot control the way the rest of the world maintains their lives, it is your responsibility to maintain yours. I am convinced that when you have a messy outward life, so goes your thought process. We serve an orderly God.

BE DETERMINED TO be happy in life! It is about choosing to be happy inside. There will always be ugly stuff and difficult people to deal with, and if you allow these things to determine your happiness, you will waiver and be unstable in all your ways. Decide to be happy—not because of people, stuff, the weather, or your finances, but because God and his promises are the source of your joy!

UNFORGIVENESS ERECTS A communication barrier between us and God. Remember that every word that God has said in the Bible he will adhere to. If you are holding unforgiveness, he says he doesn't even hear your prayer. Just imagine the price that we pay by not letting go of anger. God already knows your hurt; it is easy to just give it to him and let him deal with it. The foolish man thinks he can get by without God, but in the end, *"every knee shall bow."*

THERE ARE SO many scriptures that tell us about the joys of sharing life with others. God created us to have fellowship with him and others. *"It is not good for man to be alone."* Do not isolate yourself, and remember that *"those who have friends must show themselves friendly."* What you give out in the friend-ship area is all you will ever get back. Choose not to do life alone.

*"**HE WHO SOWS** courtesy reaps friendship, and he who plants kindness gathers love."* The way you treat others is the fruit that you will pick in your own life. Always be courteous to others. Sometimes things are said in jest, yet it is unkind. I personally will disassociate myself from a friend who feels free to insult me, even if they act like they are kidding. This behavior is usually based on jealousy and envy, and *"where there is envy and jealousy, there is also disorder and every other evil thing working."*

BY OUR OWN nature we tend to follow our own way rather than God's way. If you follow God's plan for your life, you will never get lost. Though you may stumble at times, you will not only recover from the stumble, the stumble will actually *"work toward good"* for you. If you can trust God, you can lean on his promises. No trouble can come against you when you trust his plan. There are endless possibilities available to those who completely trust God; the benefits are amazing!

Day 353   December 19

EVEN WHEN WE do our best we will still face trials and temptations, but there is always a reward that follows correct choices. God gave us the right to choose, and sometimes that choice is our biggest nemesis. He says he lays before us life and death and he tells us to choose life. While the glitz of the world may sparkle for a season, God's way brings lifetime blessings.

FAITH WITHOUT WORKS is dead. If you have a dream and are believing God for something, you have to put action with it to activate the power of faith. You have to act like your dream is actually going to come to pass. I believe one of the greatest errors that Christians make is to sit and wait for God to drop things out of the sky. God will supply your needs when you start moving.

Day 354   December 20

IF YOU WONDER what the will of God is for your life, just keep yourself busy, do what you know to be right, bless others, and then walk it out. God will direct your path like he promises. If you are trusting God, he promises that he will guide you and that your steps will be sure. Keep moving forward, knowing that the joy of life is not in the destination but in the journey.

THERE WILL BE negative issues in our lives that we will have to learn to deal with—spiritual, emotional, financial, relational, or health related. The key is to ask God for his mercy and grace to cover us as we walk out this life with all of its problems. The Scriptures say, *"His grace is sufficient."* We can handle anything if we have God's grace.

DAY 355   December 21

WHOMEVER IS HAPPY will make others happy also. Don't you just love to be around happy people? Life can be so full of trials, yet those who carry their load lightly and have a zest for living can lift others up. Choose to be that person who brings a light into every room you enter. Be the one who chooses to see the good in everyone and everything, the one who expects everything to turn out fine.

DOUBT WILL HINDER your prayers and it will come against almost everyone at one time or another. God's Word is the only real antidote for doubt, but if you don't know what it says, you do not have a spiritual weapon. When doubt comes into your mind it can be rejected, but once it gets into your heart it takes a foothold and causes you to waver. If you waver, you get nothing from God. Find promises in the Bible that cover your situation and then choose to believe them.

DAY 356   December 22

WHILE WORDS HAVE tremendous power, many times a spoken word is perceived differently than it was intended. Something is said that a listener will selectively hear, which will change the whole context of the meaning, accusing the communicator of saying something unintended. Listen to the whole subject before jumping to conclusions that can cause division. To insinuate something because you only listened to part of the conversation is nothing short of a lie. *"He who speaks before he hears is a fool and will be brought to shame."*

EVERYONE IS CREATED with the potential to do amazing things, but it is up to us as individuals to put our hands to it. God gives the potential, but we have to apply that potential to our lives. *"We are blessed according to the work of our hands."* There is no exception to that. What is your potential? Get busy and put your hands to it; do the amazing things that God created you to do.

Day 357   December 23

SUCCESS IS NOT always permanent, and failure is not fatal. The key to both is to keep moving forward. Success and failure both teach us, and true success is recognizing and implementing the lessons learned. Honor God and move ahead!

THERE WILL ALWAYS be areas in our lives where we are lacking, but God will always make it up to us somewhere else. Don't spend your time dwelling on the lack. Praise God for the blessings that surround you. Take time today to look around at all those blessings that you have been taking for granted and give proper thanks to God.

THE GREATEST MISSTEP that one can make is to think they are prettier, smarter, more important, and don't have a need for God. This is the recipe for a downward spin. No matter how much money, beauty, talent, or even fame you may have, *"be careful when you think you stand, lest you fall."* Don't think more highly of yourself than you ought. Everything can change in the blink of an eye.

"HE WHO WALKS with integrity walks securely." If you are truly doing your best to do what is right, you can rest assured that your footsteps will be secure. This does not mean you are perfect—we all make mistakes—but God knows your heart, and if you have a sincere desire to do what is right, God will protect you. Even if you stumble, the angels will catch you. There are times when it seems God's Word is not true. Remember: God works in mysterious ways; *"has he said it, and will he not do it?"*

Day 359   December 25

GOD CHOSE WORDS, both written and living, to communicate with us. Written words are powerful, but nothing touches like the sound of the human voice—especially the voice of one we love. The words we choose have within them the power of life and death. Be cognizant of frivolous words that can permanently damage a child, a marriage, a friendship, a career, and even a life. *"Kind words are like honey, sweet to the soul and healing for the whole body."* We have the ability to touch the soul of another and to bring healing to the whole body!

IF YOU WONDER what the will of God is for your life, just keep yourself moving, do what you know to be right, bless others, and walk it out. God will direct your path just like he promises. There are thousands of promises in the Bible, but if you don't know what they are, you can't claim them. I am convinced that the real difference between a life of celebration and a life of mediocrity is knowing these promises and believing them. *"Study to make yourself approved."*

DAY 360   December 26

EVEN SINCERE, GOOD people have a corrupt-ness that lives in them and tempts them to run amok. God will always show us a way out of those tempta-tions. Self-sufficiency is a great trait but it can get you into big trouble. God's Word says, *"Lean not on your own understanding, but trust in the Lord with all your heart and he will direct your path."* Don't count on yourself; instead, count on God.

GRATITUDE IS THE healthiest choice you can make. An attitude of gratitude will change your life. There are always things in life that you don't have, things to hope for, but I promise you that when you truly appreciate what you have, God will give you more. *"Delight yourself in the Lord and he will give you the desires of your heart."* Delighting yourself in the Lord is simply appreciating him and all that he has done for you. *"Seek first the kingdom of God and his righteousness and all other things shall be added unto you."*

"HE WHO HAS a slack hand becomes poor, while a diligent hand makes rich." Ultimately, it is not a get-rich-quick scheme or winning the lotto or inheriting money that will make you rich; rather, a diligent hand—a hand that keeps moving and producing, a hand that does what needs to be done and doesn't let carnage pile up around it. *"Do you see a man skilled in his work? He will stand before kings."* It doesn't matter what your work is but how well you do your work that will achieve prosperity.

HAPPINESS IS AN attitude. We choose to be happy or miserable, and choosing to act miserable takes more energy than acting happy. Life is a constant collage of ups and downs. Don't let temporary circumstances dictate your joy. "This too shall pass." Choose happiness!

DAY 362   December 28

WHEN THINGS FALL apart, we all have a choice to either break down or break through. Breaking down has absolutely no value. While there are times that tears will happen—they can even be healthy and relieve stress—don't allow yourself to wallow in your pain. A better choice is to get up and begin problem-solving. Even baby steps will move you forward toward the breakthrough that God promises those who serve him.

GOD TELLS US to find a quiet place and get rest. We are not emotionally equipped for continual action. It is so important to spend quiet time alone with God—it will draw you closer to him. No cell phones, no TV, no social media, no friends, no work—just you and God. It will sharpen your mind, increase your imagination and creativity, and your life will just be better all the way around. You will burn out if you do not take alone time. Respites are necessary for continued success.

Day 363   December 29

OUR MIND-SET CAN change our hope, hope is what activates faith in our life, and faith is what pleases God. A growth mind-set determines our progress, while a fixed mind-set does not allow us to grow and keeps us in a box. Stubborn people will never get anywhere. The mind-set we adopt in our life will determine our happiness and our success.

COMMIT YOUR LIFE to excellence. This does not mean you should be a neurotic nitpicker or a perfectionist, but it does mean you should strive for excellence in all you do. Give everything your very best and life will be sweet. There is a good feeling that abides in all of us when we know we have done our best. Even if we lose, it is still comforting to know that we did the best we could. Guilt is a horrible tormentor, but when you have done your best, guilt will never be able to catch you. *"Whatever you do, whether in word or deed, do it as unto the Lord."*

DAY 364   December 30

THE KEY TO living a successful life is knowing what to let go and what to keep. Many times we cling to the things that are actually creating the problems in our life. Things become familiar to us and even though they are not good, they are comfortable. It is wise to stop every once in a while and assess your life, examining all the aspects that make up your days. Take note of the value of each thing, and just as you would throw out an old, ugly chair, throw out the nonproductive things. Make room for the new things God wants to give you.

SOMETIMES WE FEEL like we have nothing left to give, yet these are the times God can use us most profoundly. God's Word says, *"In our weakness he is made strong."* So when you are tired, weak, frustrated, or discouraged, God has a perfect opportunity to swoop in and make things happen without us getting in his way. *"When you have done all you know to do, stand and believe."*

Day 365   December 31

THIS DAY, THIS moment and everything in it is special. Sometimes we get so busy dreaming about tomorrow or reminiscing about yesterday that we miss today. This day and all of its special effects will never happen again. Savor every moment and thank God for the gift of life. Make an intentional decision to be happy right now, right where you are.

WE SHOULD NOT be the same old person year after year. Every year we are gifted with, we should be progressing. Stubborn, foolish people refuse to expand and grow. They cling to their old ways, making the same mistakes over and over. As this year ends, stop and reflect on your takeaway. What gem did you find in the mess? Purpose in your heart to start fresh and be open to the new growth that God has planned for you, *"forgetting those things that are behind and looking to those things that are ahead."*

VELMA WAS BORN on October 11, 1942, in San Francisco, California. She grew up in Southern California and currently resides in Palm Desert, California, at the foot of the Santa Rosa Mountains. She has three children, ten grandchildren, and one great-grandchild. Prior to retiring, Velma was a successful businesswoman and now is a writer and motivational speaker. Please send inquiries, comments, and speaking requests to treasures333@yahoo.com.

Parting Thoughts...

SEEING FIRST THE DESERT SANDS
AS WANT, AS THIRST, IN NEED
DENIED THE FERTILE FIELD
THE MYRTLE TREE AND STREAMS.

AND YET THE LUPINE—IN HER HUE OF BLUE
CELEBRATES LESS SHADE IN GLORY
RISES HIGH ON SPINDLY STEM
TO SANCTIFY HER STORY.

THE VERBINIA'S SUMMER FLOWER
WITH HEATED BREATH UPON HER FACE
SENDS FORTH HER YOUTH IN TENDRILS
THE DESERT FLOOR HER SWEET EMBRACE.

T'WAS ONCE THE FERTILE FIELDS SPRING
TOMORROW'S DESERT KNOWN
YOU WILL CALL A LIFE WELL SPENT
WHEN ALL SMALL TREASURES REAPED AND SOWN.

FIND FIRST YOUR WORLD WITHIN
SHARE GENEROSITY AND SEEK
FOR AS YOU 'SEE'—YOU'LL BE
OF THOUGHT AND PROSE I SPEAK.

—Bobbi Hagar Harrell

CPSIA information can be obtained
at www.ICGtesting.com
Printed in the USA
FSHW012101110321
79363FS